U0941846

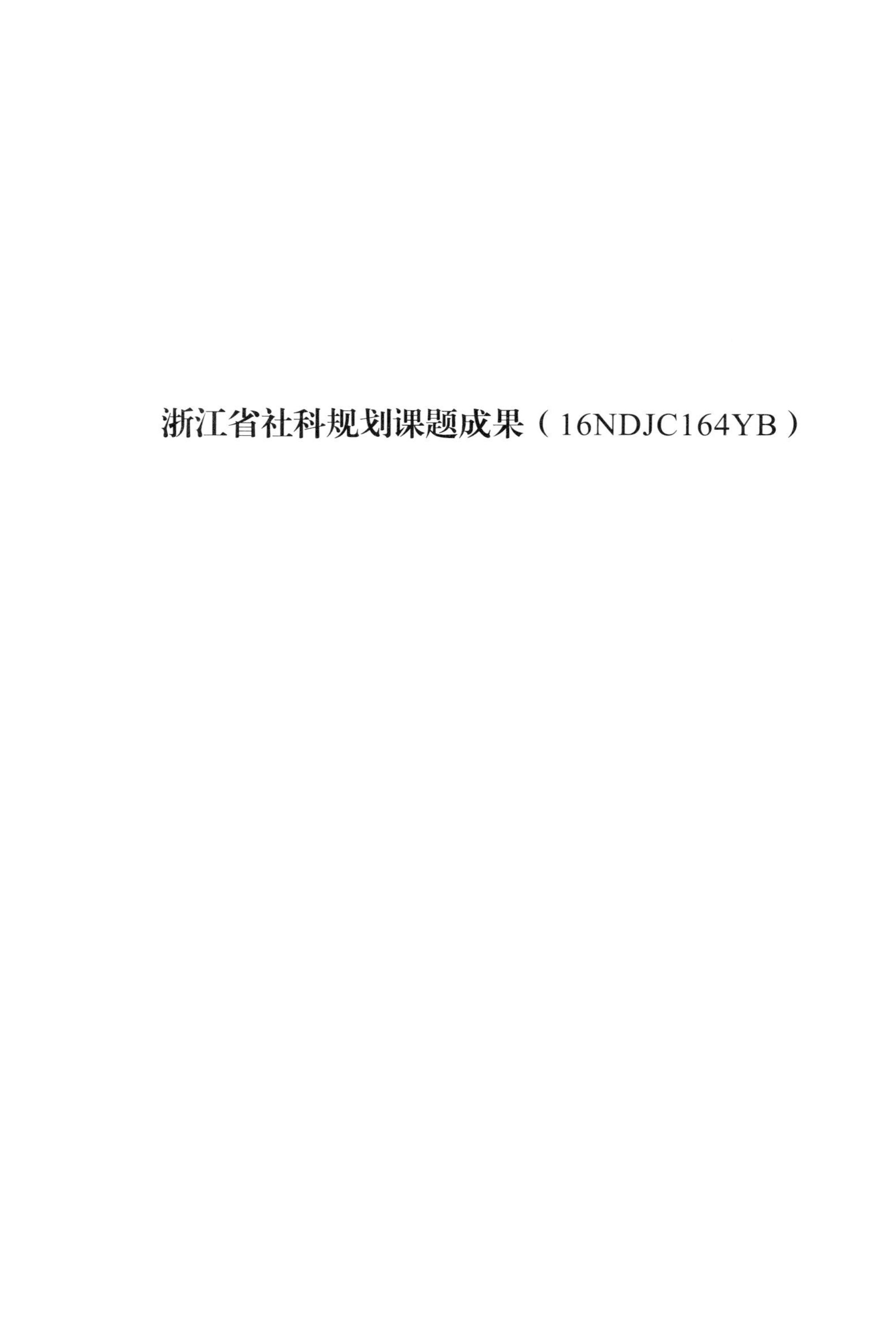

浙江省社科规划课题成果（16NDJC164YB）

英汉社会话语中的隐喻比较研究

——以政治演说为例

A Comparative Study of Metaphors in English and Chinese Social Discourse: The Case of Political Speech

柳超健◎著

中国社会科学出版社

图书在版编目(CIP)数据

英汉社会话语中的隐喻比较研究:以政治演说为例/柳超健著.
—北京:中国社会科学出版社,2018.3
ISBN 978-7-5203-2209-6

Ⅰ.①英… Ⅱ.①柳… Ⅲ.①隐喻—对比研究—英语、汉语
Ⅳ.①H15②H315

中国版本图书馆CIP数据核字(2018)第052702号

出 版 人 赵剑英
责任编辑 陈肖静
责任校对 牛 玺
责任印制 戴 宽

出 版 中国社会科学出版社
社 址 北京鼓楼西大街甲158号
邮 编 100720
网 址 http://www.csspw.cn
发 行 部 010-84083685
门 市 部 010-84029450
经 销 新华书店及其他书店

印 刷 北京明恒达印务有限公司
装 订 廊坊市广阳区广增装订厂
版 次 2018年3月第1版
印 次 2018年3月第1次印刷

开 本 710×1000 1/16
印 张 11.5
插 页 2
字 数 163千字
定 价 48.00元

To Ferry Liu

Contents

List of Figures

List of Tables

Preface

Through a comparative analysis of the conceptual metaphors identified in the political speeches by former US President Barack Obama and former Chinese President Hu Jintao, this book explores the similarities and differences between the conceptual metaphors in English and Chinese data, distills the deep causes underlying different metaphor choices on the basis of bodily and cultural experiences and proves that abstract concepts in Chinese political discourse are fundamentally metaphorical in nature. Moreover, the book considers some issues with respect to interdisciplinary research on metaphor.

Methodologically, the book divides the formal speeches from two leaders into five major categories, i. e. Address on National Independence, Address in University, Address on Earthquake Resistance and Disaster Relief, New Year Greetings and Inaugural Address. Based on the Conceptual Metaphor Theory (CMT) and a combination of quantitative and qualitative analysis, I adopt the Critical Metaphor Analysis (CMA), i. e. contextual analysis, metaphor identification, metaphor interpretation and metaphor explanation to carry out a comparative analysis of the conceptual metaphors in English and Chinese data.

In the course of the book, I strive to test the pervasiveness of conceptual metaphors in Chinese political discourse; more specifically, I clarify whether abstract concepts are partially constructed and realized in terms of conceptual metaphors in Chinese data; I then identify and analyze the typical conceptual metaphors that occur in English and Chinese data, explore the similarities and differences between the conceptual metaphors in the two languages and distill the underlying factors behind the metaphor use from the perspective of culture and embodiment. The comparative study finally shows that:

- Conceptual metaphors are pervasive in the construction of abstract concepts in Chinese political discourse.

- Abstract concepts are partially constructed and realized in terms of conceptual metaphors in Chinese political discourse. There is, however, no employment of the abstract to metaphorize the abstract or the abstract to metaphorize the concrete.

- There are HUMAN metaphor, BUILDING metaphor, JOURNEY metaphor and FAMILY metaphor both in English and Chinese data; DRAMA metaphor and RELIGIOUS metaphor are specific to English data while WAR metaphor and CIRCLE metaphor are unique in Chinese data.

- The similarities between conceptual metaphors in English and Chinese political discourse originate from human experiential bases in the physical world rather than a thin air. Since Americans and Chinese share a large part of same or similar bodily and cultural experiences which human cognition is rooted in, it comes as no surprise that we can find the shared conceptual structures both in English and Chinese data.

- Human language patterns, cultural background and linguistic worldviews strongly influence the use of conceptual metaphors such that different characteristics and features can be reflected in the metaphorical cognition of English and Chinese political languages respectively. Therefore, people from different cultural communities tend to use different metaphorical concepts in the conceptualization and categorization of the physical world.

Nick C. Lau

Yunbinwan, Powerlong

January 2018

Acknowledgements

The original title of this book is *A Comparative Study of Metaphors in English and Chinese Political Discourse*, but I need to make a compromise and get the title changed due to some unspeakable and you-know-what-I-mean reasons. Fortunately, there are still the people in my life that encourage me to move forward and persevere till the destination.

First and foremost, I would like to dedicate this book to my supervisor Liu Fagong, without whose patient guidance, insightful suggestions, fatherly encouragement and exceptional support, a study in this discipline would not have been completed in reasonable time.

I also appreciate the scholarly help I have received from Chai Gaiying, Chen Mingyao, Fan Zhenqiang, Jia Aiwu, Pan Zhangxian, Shang Biwu, Wang Lei, Wang Shuwen and Yang Xianju, whose teaching and lecturing are of great significance to the fulfillment of this research. But their help of course means a lot more for me than just taking scholarly advice.

Special thanks are given to Liu Yuhong at Nanjing Normal University, Lai Yan and Qian Yufang at Communication University of Zhejiang, Lin Youmiao, Zhang Qi and Zhu Changhe at Huzhou University, Zhejiang province, for their continued encouragement and care all the time.

This book would not have been possible without grants from Zhejiang Federation of Humanities and Social Sciences Circles (grant number: NDJC164YB), Postgraduate Research and Practice Innovation Program of Jiangsu Province(grant number: KYCX17_1965) (I am especially grateful to my supervisor Wang Jun and my brother Wang Xiaoping at Soochow University, for their help with the application process), Scientific Research Program (ZC17XJ024) and English Language and Literature of Communication University of Zhejiang where I have had the privilege of teaching for the past years.

Chen Xiaojing, the beautiful lady at China Social Sciences Press is exceptionally helpful and supportive at all stages in the publication of this book.

Finally, I would like to extend my deepest gratitude to my family, for the endless love and support in other ways.

Nick C. Lau

Yunbinwan, Powerlong

January 2018

List of Abbreviations

CMT Conceptual Metaphor Theory

CMA Critical Metaphor Analysis

MIP Metaphor Identification Procedure

Chapter 1　Introduction

1.1　Some preliminaries

Let me just begin by reflecting on the key concept of this book *metaphor*. By 'metaphor' I mean the phenomenon whereby we talk about, potentially, understand, experience and even reason about one kind of thing in terms of another (Lakoff & Johnson, 1980: 5; Semino, 2008: 1). For example, in the linguistic expression 'long, rugged path towards prosperity and freedom', we can see that a nation's rising and development is talked about in terms of a long journey that involves some form of short-term suffering or struggle, which may reinforce a particular but perfectly reasonable way of thinking and even reasoning about the cause in terms of a PATH schema.

The common knowledge is that languages are dependent on human thoughts, and the processing of human thoughts is inseparable from the conceptual judgment and logical reasoning as well. To reveal the nature of language, we need to analyze and make sense of the cognitive subjects' way of thinking through the use of their languages. Moreover, dialectical materialism theorists hold that people's social existence determines their social consciousness and that people's way of thinking is closely related to their behavioral patterns which at least include the mode of social existence, the personal experience, and the social and cultural patterns. In fact, metaphor studies mainly deal with the complex relationships between people's way of thinking and their behavioral patterns in that metaphor is pervasive in everyday life, not just in language but in thought and action, and our ordinary conceptual system, in terms of which we both think and act, is fundamentally metaphorical in nature (Lakoff & Johnson, 1980: 1; Xie, 2007: preface). The following is an example of such a set (Lakoff & Johnson, 1980: 4).

Your claims are *indefensible*.
He *attacked every weak point* in my argument.
His criticisms were *right on target*.
I *demolished* his argument.
I've never *won* an argument with him.
You disagree? Okay, *shoot*!
If you use that *strategy*, he'll *wipe you out*.
He *shot down* all of my arguments.

Given all these sentences, we may note that a large part of the way we speak about argument or debate in English derives from the way we speak about war. Technically, some elements in the concrete conceptual domain 'war' equipped with a highly organized structure get mapped onto the elements in the relatively abstract conceptual domain 'argument' without a systematic structure. Within CMT, an important distinction needs to be implicitly introduced between metaphorical expression, such as 'shoot down' and its corresponding conceptual metaphor or metaphorical concept ARGUMENT IS WAR. The metaphorical expressions in italics above that come from the language or terminology of the more concrete conceptual domain are named as linguistic metaphor①. The conventional patterns of concept underlying the metaphorical expressions are labeled as conceptual metaphor. The former is the specific linguistic realization of the latter. Thus, all the linguistic expressions in italics that have to do with argument and that come from the domain of war are linguistic metaphors, whereas the conceptual metaphor that these linguistic metaphors make manifest is ARGUMENT IS WAR.

1.2 Rationale and hypotheses

Metaphor has been a popular area of study for a long history, which could probably be traced back to the time of Aristotle in ancient Greece. Within that tradition, metaphor was typically treated as a device of the poetic imagination and the rhetorical flourish. It is a matter of extraordinary language use beyond the reach of someone who just talks, rather than human thought or action in everyday functioning. Specifically, metaphorical expressions were assumed to be mutually exclusive with the realm of ordinary everyday language: everyday language had no metaphor, and metaphor used mechanisms outside the realm of everyday conventional language (Lakoff, 1993).

However, with the emergence of cognitive linguistics, especially since the publication of the book *Metaphors We Live By* coauthored by Lakoff and Johnson (1980), a growing number of scholars both in and

① In this book, linguistic metaphors, metaphorically used words, metaphor related words and metaphorical expressions are treated as the same concept in metaphor identification.

out this scope have started to cast a cognitive light on the study of metaphor, accepting that metaphor is not just a rhetorical tool or a linguistic phenomenon, but a way of human thinking, and that metaphor plays an important role in everyday language and social activities and it acts as a powerful cognitive tool for human categorization and conceptualization of the physical world. The recent work of this field includes Lakoff & Johnson (1980a, 1980b, 1999), Kövecses (1986, 1990, 2000, 2005, 2010), Johnson (1987, 2007), Lakoff (1987, 1993), Lakoff & Turner (1989), Taylor (1989), Turner (1990, 1992, 1993, 2000), Croft (1993), Glucksberg & Keysar (1993), Zhao (1994, 1998, 2001), Yu (1995, 1998, 2003), Fauconnier (1997), Goatly (1997, 2007), Grady (1997), Lin (1997), Shu (1998, 2000, 2003), Wang Y (2000, 2004, 2006, 2008), Fauconnier & Turner (2002), Koller (2002, 2004), Shu & Tang (2002), Lan (2003, 2005), Li & Liu (2003), Littlemore (2003), Ritchie (2003, 2013), Wang W (2003, 2006, 2007), Hu (2004), Gibbs (2006, 2008), Littlemore & Low (2006), Tang (2007), Wei (2007), Xie (2007), Wang & Wang (2008). Therefore, it can be suggested that contemporary metaphor research has basically transferred from the traditional rhetoric into many other areas and disciplines, such as psychology, philosophy, anthropology, sociology, linguistics, literary criticism, cognitive science, translation and so on.

If metaphors are not just rhetoric ornaments, but a way of human thinking, there is then no reason why this potential could be only used to structure the concepts underlying certain abstract words, and why it could not show up in the way we approach the complex scientific, political and social issues of the world (Ungerer & Schmid, 2008: 144 - 5). After all, language is a tool, and a process of human perception and description of the world (Pan, 2001: 28). Metaphor then can be applied to many aspects of social activities in which politics is what we would expect metaphorical expressions to be used since the top purpose of political rhetoric is persuasion, or, more bluntly, the creation of political myth among people.

Since 1970s, there has been a number of prior work on metaphor in political discourse, which covers the exploration of the nature, mechanism and working process of metaphorical cognition. For example, Lakoff (1991, 2002, 2003, 2004, 2006a, 2006b, 2008), Miller (1992), Graber (1993), Chilton (1996, 2004), Mio (1997), Li (2000), Wang & Li (2003), Charteris-Black (2004, 2011, 2014), Musolff (2004, 2006, 2016), Huang (2006), Zhu (2007), Cao (2008), Chen & Liu (2009), Huang & Wu (2009), He (2011, 2014), Wu & Pang (2011), Wang J(2012), Wang & Yang (2012), Wu (2012, 2016), Wang S(2014), Wen (2014), Liang (2015), Liang & Wang (2015), Wang & Zhang (2017). However, due attention has not yet been given to a systematic comparative study of conceptual metaphors in the background of different political languages. The reason is that most scholars in China show great enthusiasm for the introduction of western metaphor theories, and yet, they tend to neglect the comparative study of metaphor in English and Chinese based on the theories they advocated. Consequently, the potential values of these theories have not been fully explored (Liu, 2008: 25).

So, an important and urgent study in this scope is to conduct a systematic comparative research on metaphor based on other languages rather than English within different discourse patterns, such that it would be possible to test whether abstract thoughts are partially constructed and realized in terms of metaphorical reference in these languages. Thus, the following hypotheses could be proposed:

• Since human social activities are deeply rooted in their bodily and cultural experiences, of which people from different cultural communities share a large part, we may assume that the universality of metaphor holds true in different political languages.

• There should be some variations in the conceptual system of people from different cultures as human experiential bases are not excluded from their specific social and cultural patterns. Specifically, it is the concrete conceptual domains with highly organized structures that get mapped onto the relatively abstract conceptual domains which do not possess systematic structures in political languages, although Wang W (2003; 2007) suggests that there is not only the use of the concrete to evoke the abstract in Chinese, but also the employment of the concrete to metaphorize the concrete, the abstract to metaphorize the concrete and the abstract to metaphorize the abstract.

1.3 Research questions

With a comparative analysis of the conceptual metaphors identified in the public speeches by former US President Barack Obama and former Chinese President Hu Jintao, this book focuses specifically on the following questions:

• It has been proved that metaphor is pervasive in English political language, is it still the case in Chinese political discourse?

• It has been argued that abstract concepts are partially constructed and realized in terms of conceptual metaphors in English political speeches, does it hold true in Chinese political speeches? Are there other realizations?

- What typical conceptual metaphors occur in the two languages?
- What similarities and differences are there between the conceptual metaphors in English and Chinese political discourse?
- What explanations are there of the similarities and differences?

1.4 Research significance

1.4.1 Theoretical significance

This book not only strengthens the scientificity of a number of prior work within CMT, which benefits its application and development in a range of interdisciplinary studies, but it is a bold attempt to test the feasibility of CMT for guiding practice. While metaphor in politics has featured in numerous academic articles both in and out cognitive linguistics, to date there is few research that gives a comparative study of conceptual metaphors in English and Chinese political discourse. Therefore, this book promotes the development of comparative study of political language in English and Chinese.

1.4.2 Practical implications

This book enriches our understanding of political languages by revealing how political myth is created to express specific attitudes and evaluations, and how political metaphors are construed to highlight or hide ideology and cultural stereotypes. Thus, it contributes to the future research on politics and culture both in English and Chinese and provides important reference for cross-cultural communication, language teaching and translation (e. g. corresponding transfer of conceptual metaphors in different languages and cultures). What is more, it sheds some new light on comparative study in other interdisciplinary field. In brief, what the book strives for is an informed reading of metaphorical concepts in political discourse.

1.5 The structure of this book

The book is organized into six chapters as follows:

Chapter 1 serves as an introduction to the book, including some preliminaries, rationale, hypotheses, research questions, research significance and the structure.

Chapter 2 is concerned with a comprehensive literature review of the prior work on metaphor in political language, which is then followed by a detailed description of the relationship between metaphor and politics, metaphor and ideology, metaphor and political persuasion and finally a general overview of the research on political metaphors both at home and abroad.

Chapter 3 mainly deals with the research methodology, data collection and research procedure where I explain an approach what Charteris-Black describes as Critical Metaphor Analysis.

Chapter 4 and 5 constitute the body part of the book that is devoted to data description and comparative analysis of the text samples respectively. The major task of chapter 4 focuses specifically on the identification, interpretation and explanation of conceptual metaphors in English and Chinese political languages. In chapter 5 a comparative analysis is conducted between conceptual metaphors identified in the two different political languages.

Chapter 6 provides some conclusions to the book as a whole, including the major findings, implications and limitations of the study. The prospects for future research are also discussed as well.

Chapter 2 Literature Review

The present chapter is intended to provide a comprehensive review of the previous work with reference to conceptual metaphors in political discourse. I begin by introducing the historical background of such different approaches to metaphor studies as the linguistic approach, the pragmatic approach, the interactionist approach and the cognitive approach, and then go on to consider the links between metaphor and politics, metaphor and ideology, metaphor and political persuasion and finally present a general overview of the prior research on political metaphors both at home and abroad.

2.1 The historical background of different approaches to metaphor

In the western tradition, there have been many different approaches to metaphor: the traditional linguistic approach considers metaphor as a deviant phenomenon in language which produces either a false statement or an ungrammatical sentence in order to reveal similarities that could have been as easily expressed literally; the pragmatic approach takes metaphor as a special act, to make sense out of which calls for a special set of principles; the interactionist approach understands metaphor as an interaction between two subjective systems and finally the cognitive approach views metaphor as conceptual mapping from the source domain to the target domain (Lan, 2003: 5). In what follows I will review these different approaches briefly.

2.1.1 The linguistic approach

The traditional linguistic approach to metaphor is mainly represented by two theories: the comparison theory and the substitution theory. The substitution theory is any view which argues that a metaphorical expression is used in place of an equivalent literal expression and, therefore, is completely replaceable by its literal counterpart. Metaphor, then, involves a substitution of an improper word for the proper one (Way, 1991: 33).

The linguistic view is basically consistent with Aristotle's claim that metaphor consists in giving the thing a name that belongs to something else; the transference being either from genus to species, or from species to genus, or from species to species, or on grounds of analogy (*Poetics* 1457 b: 6 – 9), and that the greatest thing by far is to have a command of metaphor and that this alone cannot be imparted to another: it is the mark of genus, for to make a good metaphor implies an eye for resemblances (*Poetics* 1459 a: 3 – 8). His interpretation of metaphor as a transference of names later was, for the most part, replaced by a more sophisticated form known as the comparison theory.

The substitution theory views metaphor as a rhetorical substitution of literal expressions and only a rhetorical decoration device. Although some insights into the nature of metaphor could be obtained from the substitution theory, it is unable to walk out of the shadow of Aristotle's view in that metaphor is also treated as something abnormal in language as well in this theory. The status of metaphor on the substitution view is that of mere ornamentation: an author chooses to use it instead of a literal equivalent for reasons of style and decoration. Thus, metaphor has no special significance in this view except as a method of making literal speech fancier and more appealing. However, the comparison theory is more sophisticated than that of mere substitution because the comparison view holds that metaphor is comparing two things for similarity rather than just substituting terms. Thus, a metaphor becomes an elliptical simile, that is, a collapsed literal comparison from which the 'like' or 'as' has simply been omitted. This view also maintains that the meaning of any metaphoric expression can still be completely captured by a literal equivalent, as long as the literal expression is one of explicit comparison. Thus, when we say 'men are wolves' we are really saying 'men are like wolves', which means we take all the characteristics of men and all the characteristics of wolves and compare them for similarities. The similarities found between the tenor, in this case 'men', and vehicle, 'wolves', become the ground of the metaphor (Way, 1991: 34).

The comparison theory is the best example of the objectivists orientation toward metaphor. It holds that literal concepts and propositions have meaning only insofar as they can map onto mind-independence realities existing objectively in the world. It treats literal meaning as basic and fundamental. Thus, whatever meaning a metaphorical expression has must consist of a set of literal similarity statements. It is only via this literal core of meaning that a metaphor has any cognitive function at all. It follows, therefore, that metaphors have no role in the generation of experiential structure; instead, they can, at best, be only secondary devices for indirectly reporting on preexisting objective states of affairs

(Johnson, 1987: 67).

2.1.2 The pragmatic approach

There have been several different attempts at a pragmatic approach to metaphor, among which Goatly (1997) introduces Sperber and Wilson's (1986) Relevance Theory as a framework for understanding the pragmatic processes involved in recognizing and understanding metaphor. According to him, metaphorical understanding depends on the processes involved in the interplay between knowledge of the language system, knowledge of the context, and background schematic knowledge about the world and the society (Lan, 2003: 8); metaphor is not a product of a breakaway from the normal language or a violation of the principles of communication. The meaning of metaphor is a loose talk which belongs to the visualized expression in varieties that does not violate any principle of communication (He & Ran, 2002: 222). Thus, metaphor requires no special interpretive abilities or procedures: it is a natural outcome of some very general abilities and procedures used in verbal communication.

Later, a more systematic pragmatic approach to metaphor can be found in Searle's research. In Searle's treatment of metaphor, he views metaphor as a speech act and the sentence means one thing ('S is P'), but the speaker's meaning is something different ('S is R'), where 'S is R', the meaning the speaker has in mind, is the metaphoric meaning, and thus has a definite cognitive content; moreover, and most important, the interpreter of the metaphor must somehow recover this content. In its simplest form, the question he is trying to answer is how is it possible for the speaker to say metaphorically 'S is P' and mean 'S is R', when P plainly does not mean R? How is it possible for the hearer who hears the utterance 'S is P' to know that the speaker means 'S is R'? (Levinson, 1992: 115)

At first glance, it appears that Searle has a straightforward "literal-core" theory, for both the sentence meaning (of 'S is P') and the intended speaker's meaning (of 'S is R') are literal. However, Searle makes it very clear that every literal utterance ultimately presupposes a nonrepresentational, nonpropositional, preintentional 'Background' of capacities, skills, and instance in order to determine its conditions of satisfaction. The meaning of any metaphor will be determined only against a preintentional background that cannot be represented propositionally (Johnson, 1987: 72).

2.1.3 The interactionist approach

I. A. Richards is one of the scholars making unique contributions to the study of metaphor in the early 20th century. In the work *The Philosophy of Rhetoric*, he argues that thought is irreducibly metaphorical and that linguistic metaphors are the specific realizations of these underlying metaphorical thought processes. He also suggests that our world is a projected world and that the processes of metaphor in language, the exchanges between the meanings of words which we study in explicit verbal metaphors, are superimposed upon a perceived world which is itself a product of earlier or unwitting metaphor, and we shall not deal with them justly if we forget that this is so (Richards, 1936: 108 –9). Moreover, he puts out that "metaphor is the omnipresent principle of language" and emphasizes that "we cannot get through three sentences of ordinary fluid discourse without metaphor". Even in the rigid language of the settled sciences we do not eliminate or prevent it without great difficulty (ibid: 92). Richards' view on metaphor thus turns out to be a breakthrough of cognitive perspective on metaphor.

Later, Black develops Richards' interaction theory and states that metaphors may serve as "cognitive instruments", which are indispensable for perceiving connections that, once perceive, and then truly present (Black, 1962: 37). In summary, the main points from Black's interaction view of metaphor are: metaphor involves entire systems of assumptions and 'commonplaces' which are associated with the terms involved; that the metaphorical process works like a filter, with the associated ideas of the secondary subject (vehicle) hiding, highlighting and organizing aspects of the primary subject; understanding metaphor often involves a shift in meaning; metaphor cannot be reduced to any literal statements of comparison, and; metaphor can actually create similarity between previously dissimilar ideas (Way, 1991: 48).

Black argues that there is a class of metaphors with irreducible meaning above and beyond any statement of literal similarities between two objects. Such metaphors do not work merely by projecting discrete properties of one object or event onto another object or event that shares those properties. For example, both the concepts of time and money are thought to share the property of being quantifiable over discrete units. But the meaning of TIME IS MONEY is not simply a list of such properties and relations shared by both time and money. Instead, the meaning of the metaphor depends on thought processes in which an entire system of implications from the domain of money interacts with the implicative system of the domain of time (Johnson, 1987: 70).

In addition, a few other scholars have also inherited the tradition and developed this theory. For example, Mac (1990) offers a formal explanation for metaphor by using the Fuzzy Set Theory; Indurkhya (1992) sets up a new concise framework which can explain how a metaphor creates similarities between its two components. By maintaining that metaphor is an omnipresent phenomenon of language and highlighting the interaction between the two components of metaphor, the interaction view has begun to recognize the cognitive value of metaphor and has paved a way for the emergence of a brand new cognitive approach (Lan, 2003: 12).

2.1.4 The cognitive approach

The contemporary theory that metaphor is primarily conceptual, conventional, and part of the ordinary conceptual system of thought and language can be traced to Michael Reddy's paper *The Conduit Metaphor* in which he proposes that the locus of metaphor is thought, not language, that metaphor is a major and indispensable part of our ordinary, conventional way of conceptualizing the world, and that our everyday behavior reflects our metaphorical understanding of experience. Though other theorists had noticed some of these characteristics of metaphor, Reddy was the first to demonstrate it by rigorous linguistic analysis, stating generalizations over voluminous examples (Lakoff, 1993).

However, the work which marks the establishment of the cognitive approach to metaphor is Lakoff and Johnson's work *Metaphors We Live By* (1980), the major claims of which have basically turned the study of metaphor into a new page, shifting away from the ornamental device and the linguistic fact to the cognitive nature, extending metaphorical process into the realm of human perception and cognition and viewing metaphor as a base to human existence. For the past decades, the cognitive approach to metaphor has been developed by Lakoff and his colleagues in a larger number of researches (Lakoff & Johnson, 1980, 1999; Kövecses, 1986, 1990; Lakoff, 1987, 1993; Lakoff & Tuner

1989; Turner, 1992, 1993). The basic claims of this approach can be summarized along the following lines (Lan, 2003: 31):

- Metaphor is ubiquitous: it is pervasive in everyday life, not just in language but in thought and action.
- Metaphor is conceptual in nature.
- Metaphor is systematic.
- Metaphor is composed of two domains, a relatively more clearly structured source domain and a relatively less clearly structured target domain.
- Metaphorical mappings are not arbitrary but are grounded in our bodily experience.

2.2 Metaphor and politics

The world of politics is complex, value-laden and both cognitively and perceptually removed from the immediacy of everyday experience. The dynamics and consequences of politics are neither tangible, self-evident, nor simple (Thompson, 1996: 185 - 6). The domain of 'politics' is, therefore, not easy to define or delimit (Semino, 2008: 85). Politics is also about the organization of social relationships, about power, influence, the balance between autonomy and community, about trade-offs between contradictory needs and values, which are all reflected in political discourses, in the metaphors people use and the stories they tell (Ritchie, 2013: 161). Metaphorical processes are one of the most important means by which human minds form concepts of, and reason about, their spatial and temporal environments. This is especially the case for conceptualization of abstract, unfamiliar, or complex domains. Such domains include, for instance, social and political institutions, international relations, strategic doctrines (Chilton, 1996: 48).

Since political discourse is rather complex and abstract, and far from people's everyday realities, and therefore the use of different metaphors on the part of politicians tends to link the individual and the political by providing a way of seeing relations, reifying abstractions, and framing complexity in manageable terms (Thompson, 1996: 185 – 6). In other words, a general function of conceptual metaphors in political discourse is to simplify abstract and complex concepts so as to make them accessible to the public.

However, in order to reveal and explain the use of metaphors in political discourse, we need to consider a number of more specific functions that metaphors may have in communication. The recent emphasis on the persuasiveness and centrality of metaphor in both language and thought has led to more comprehensive accounts of the role of metaphor in politics, which includes both its uses in political discourse and its functions in the cognitive processes and representations that are involved in the production and reception of political texts (Semino, 2008: 86).

Thompson (1996), for example, argues that human needs metaphor to do and think about politics through the metaphor 'fish needs water to be fish', namely, metaphor is the very stuff and substance of political discourse and the choice of a particular metaphor really matters. Chilton (1996) explains in detail how the choice of particular metaphors could contribute to shape the dominant view of international politics in the USA and its allied countries during the time of the Cold War. Politicians do this through a process of highlighting some aspects of a political issues and at the same time hiding other aspects by putting them into the background. Nimmo and Coombs (1987) maintain that if metaphors are necessary for elites and policy makers as essential simplifications and clarifications and necessary devices to bridge the gap between general policy goals and values and the concrete means, they are even more necessary and important for general observers and occasional participants in politics. Charteris-Black (2004) shows how metaphors used by successful political leaders explain the association between conscious beliefs and unconscious emotion in order to project the benefits that arises from their leadership and the dangers that come with that of their counterparts. The conceptual projection is usually achieved by the creation of good intention, good thinking and sounding right with subliminal use of conceptual metaphors.

2.3 Metaphor and ideology

Metaphors are seldom neutral (Semino, 2008: 32). Therefore, the fact that we talk and, potentially, even reason about something in terms of something else leads to a wide range of unique but specific attitudes and evaluations of 'something' in question. Within CMT, the very systematicity of metaphors could highlight one aspect of the target domain and hide others. For example, the conceptual metaphor ARGUMENT IS WAR highlights the aggressive, confrontational aspects of argument and keeps us from focusing on their cooperative, constructive aspects that are inconsistent with that metaphor. This may affect not just our ways of talking and thinking about arguments, but possibly even the ways we act in the midst of a heated argument (Lakoff & Johnson, 1980: 10). Specifically, the choice of one metaphor rather than another has consequences for how a particular issue is 'framed' or structured, which aspects are foregrounded and which backgrounded, what inferences are facilitated, what evaluative and emotional associations triggered, what courses of action appear to be possible and so on (Semino, 2008: 91). This finding points to one fact that when particular uses of metaphor become the dominant way of thinking about a particular aspect of reality within a particular discourse, they may be extremely difficult to perceive and challenge, since they come to represent the 'commonsense' or 'natural' view of things. In such cases, conventional conceptual metaphors can be seen as an important part of the shared sets of beliefs, or 'ideology' (ibid: 33).

Ideology is a system of beliefs and values that are based on a set of cognitive models, i. e. mental representations-partly linguistic, partly non-linguistic-of recurrent phenomena and their interpretations in culture and society (Dirven et al, 2003: 1 - 2). They then argue that it is not simply the choice of a particular conceptual metaphor that determines the ideological perspectives, but also, and equally decisively, the various linguistic expressions instantiating the underlying conceptual metaphors (ibid: 8). Van Dijk (1998: 46) similarly views ideology as the basis of the social representations shared by members of group that include scripts, scenarios, frames, attitudes, opinions and so on. Semino (2008: 90) treats ideologies as cognitive phenomena, i. e. as shared conceptualizations of particular aspects of reality, which include conventional conceptual metaphors alongside other long-term mental representations. In CMT term, many of the shared metal representations are structured, at least in part, via conventional conceptual metaphors (ibid: 33).

For example, Koller (2004) shows how business media discourse is represented by systematic metaphorical concepts that draw from a number of source domains such as 'war', 'sport', 'marriage', 'game' and so on. She then argues that the use of such metaphorical concepts reflects a sexist ideology shared by journalists and audiences, namely, business activities are treated as aggressive, competitive and antagonistic, where women tend to be marginalized.

The ideological purpose of metaphor is its systematic use in a way that forms long-term mental representations which contribute to a particular view of the world that can be described as a political myth (Charteris-Black, 2014: 211). For example, Lakoff (2002) explores in detail the ideologies of two Parties in US by comparing two different moral systems, namely, STRICT FATHER model and NURTURANT PARENT model, based on which he claims that Republicans use metaphors that emphasize government's authority and power, while Democrats use metaphors that emphasize the caring role of government.

In many cases, metaphor choice is motivated by ideology. The same notions could have been communicated in a different way if the ideology had been different and the same metaphors can be employed in different ways according to ideological perspectives. In politics, for example, WAR metaphor could be used either to attack an opponent's point of view or to represent the opponent as an aggressor. Different aspects of the source domain were found to correspond with different ideological outlooks (ibid: 247). Therefore, conventional conceptual metaphors can be an important element of ideologies and are the bread and butter of political language (Semino, 2008: 90; Charteris-Black, 2014: 28).

2.4 Metaphor and political persuasion

One of the main ways in which power can be gained, maintained or undermined is by affecting others' views and behavior, i. e. by getting others to hold views that are advantageous to a particular individual, group or cause. The general rhetorical goal of persuasion is central to much political action, and language is one of the main tool for the achievement of this general goal. It is therefore not surprising that language plays a central role in politics, and that much political action is, either wholly or partly, linguistic action (Semino, 2008: 85).

Persuasion is about being right and only once the speaker has convinced the audience that he is right can the audience be said to have been persuaded. A prerequisite for being right is that the speaker gains trust by establishing his ethical integrity. The way that trust is established is by convincing the audience that the leader has the right intensions for the group and that he has their interests heart (Charteris-Black, 2014: 14).

Metaphor is a powerful linguistic and conceptual tool for the achievement of persuasion. In political rhetoric, the primary purpose of metaphors is to frame how we view or understand political issues by eliminating alternative points of view. Politician use metaphors for negative representation of states of affairs that are construed as problematic and positive representations of future scenarios that are construed as solutions to problems. Therefore, they combine the rhetoric of right thinking with sounding right and having the right intentions (ibid: 32 – 3).

Metaphor is a figure of speech and an effective means for politician to develop persuasive political myths and arguments by applying what is familiar, and already experienced, to new topics to demonstrate that they are thinking rationally about political issues. This is because it represents a certain mental representation that reflects a shared system of belief as to what the world is and cultural-specific beliefs about mankind's place in it. It offers a way of looking at the world that may differ from the way we normally look at it and, as a result, offers some fresh insight. Because of this cognitive and culturally rooted role, metaphor is important in influencing emotional responses (ibid: 44).

2.5 Prior research on political metaphors at home and abroad

In the western rhetorical tradition, the research on political metaphor can be traced back to the writings of classical rhetoricians such as Aristotle in ancient Greek. Since 1980s, the research on metaphor from the perspective of cognition and mind has been witnessed in numerous directions. Almost at the same time, metaphorical analysis has been also applied to many different areas, such as anthropology, architecture, economics, geography, philosophy, psychology, religion, and sociology (Beer & Landtsheer, 2004). In what follows, we shall focus on those typical work on political metaphors both at home and abroad.

Howe (1988) points out that the metaphors used in contemporary American political discourse draw heavily and systematically from the terminology of sports and warfare. These sources provide metaphors for use in both campaign rhetoric and the jargon of political professionals. By studying the use of these metaphors in the period 1980 – 1985, he concludes that politics is typically conceived of as being either a rule-bound context (SPORTS metaphors) or as an unpredictable exercise of power (WAR metaphors). These metaphors are deeply rooted in American culture and appeal widely to the American electorate, but they draw on experience more commonly shared by American males than by American females. Such metaphors may have the effect of excluding women from participating in the dominant discourse of politics and thus from achieving political power.

Semino and Masci (1996) examine the use of a set of recurring metaphors in the discourse of Silvio Berlusconi, the media tycoon who became Italy's Prime Minister in 1994. They focus specifically on metaphors drawn from the source domains of football, war and the Bible. Within CMT, they consider the possible effects that each metaphorical connection may have on Berlusconi's audience in the specific political and cultural context within which he operates. They then argue that Berlusconi adopts different metaphors in an attempt to alter the way in which Italians relate to politics, to create a positive public image for himself and his new political Party and to attract particular sections of the electorate. Thus, they conclude that metaphor is an essential part of a new type of populist and heterogeneous political discourse that Berlusconi has introduced in Italian politics.

Thompson (1996) discusses over the necessity of metaphors in political discourse, exploring the consequences of metaphorical language for political participants, examining the role of metaphors for elites, and dealing with the paradoxical role of metaphors in the political life of the mass public whose relation to politics ranges from casual interest and voting to alienation and apathy. Moreover, he argues that metaphors can make politics accessible to average citizens and induce acquiescence and passivity.

Goatly (2002) investigates the use of metaphors for education in the Hong Kong Special Administrative Region's (SAR) educational reform proposals by analysis of the government's Review of Education System Reform Proposals. He discovers six or seven major metaphorical schemata for education, namely, commodity acquisition, mechanism, building construction, a path or journey of exploration, growth and nurture, with a subschema of catering. In addition, he suggests that the reforms are intended to encourage internal motivation in students that will lead to their creating knowledge and to their all-round development, and the metaphorical schemata are evaluated in terms of whether they tend to reinforce or undermine these goals and that growth/nurture and journey of exploration tend to reinforce the goals of the reforms, building construction and paths seem to be neutral or ambiguous, whereas commodity acquisition, mechanism, and catering would appear to undermine them. He also considers the ways in which metaphorical interactions can lead to confused thinking and argument.

Deason and Gonzales (2012) examine the 2008 presidential Party convention acceptance speeches from the perspective of George Lakoff's theory of moral politics, which argues that a metaphor of the nation as a family guides the adoption of a political ideology and facilitates persuasion. They coded speeches for instantiations of Strict Father and Nurturant Parent morality and for the social and political issues. They found, as expected, that Democrats referenced more Nurturant Parent themes than Strict Father themes but that Republicans used instantiations from both moral worldviews at similar rates. Democrats, but not Republicans, framed Party-owned issues in terms of their corresponding moral worldview.

Lakoff is a prolific scholar in the research on metaphor in politics. He (1980) argues that each metaphor could highlight certain aspects of a concept and implicitly hide others. Metaphors are employed for hiding some intentions that the politicians do not want to exposure in public.

Since early 1990s, Lakoff has widened the scope of his politically oriented cognitive analysis in attempt to capture different worldviews of American Conservatives and Liberals. In *Moral Politics* (2002), based on two contrasting cognitive models of family, the STRICT FATHER model and the NURTURANT PARENT model, he analyzes the unconscious worldviews of liberals and conservatives and explains why they are at odds over so many seemingly unrelated issues. The differences, he argues, are not mere matters of partisanship, but arise from radically different conceptions of morality and ideal family life. Although Lakoff stresses the objectivity of his analysis in metaphor, we may still get his preferences and find that he is concerned about the rise of Conservatism in the US during the last decade.

Since September 11 attacks, the Bush administration has relentlessly invoked the word 'freedom', using it to justify everything from preemptive strikes on Iraq to the privatization of Social Security. Yet many Democrats see President Bush's use of the word as meaningless and opportunistic – and ultimately leading to the curtailment of the very freedoms he claims to support. Furthermore, Lakoff's *Whose Freedom* (2006) reveals the ways in which language and repetition in the media have been used to enact a devastating, calculated redefinition of freedom.

Lakoff's *The Political Mind* (2008) follows on the heels of his book *The Political Mind: You Can't Understand 21st Century American Politics with an 18th Century Brain*, *Thinking Points* (2006) and *Don't Think of an Elephant* (2004), all of which focus on how politicians employ language to frame their arguments. Lakoff spells out what cognitive science has discovered about reason, and reveals that human reason is far more interesting than we thought it was. Reason is physical, mostly unconscious, metaphorical, emotion-laden, and tied to empathy. There are biological explanations behind our moral and political thought processes. His call for a New Enlightenment is a bold and striking challenge to the cherished beliefs not only of philosophers, but of pundits, pollsters, and political leaders.

In the work *Metaphor and Political Discourse: Analogical Reasoning in Debates about Europe*, Musolff (2004) conducts a systematic analysis of the function of metaphor in political discourse on the basis of the material from an extensive corpus of British and German press coverage of EU politics between 1989 and 2001. The analysis of distributions of "metaphor scenarios" in the two corpus samples reveals the differences in attitude and argumentative tendencies and leads to a refinement of cognitive metaphor theory by systematically relating conceptual, semantic and argumentation levels and incorporating the historical dimension of metaphor evolution. Finally, by drawing on examples of metaphor negotiation and on a reassessment of Hobbes' concept of metaphor in Leviathan, he highlights the ethical dimension of metaphors in politics.

In *Corpus Approaches to Critical Metaphor Analysis*, Charteris-Black (2004) adopts corpus approaches to critically analyze metaphors in various discourses by unifying the traditional, pragmatic and cognitive approaches to metaphor. He explains why metaphors are persuasive and suggests that they should be ideologically effective because they are cognitively plausible and evoke an emotional response. Under the framework of his Critical Metaphor Analysis, Charteris-Black makes a systematic comparative analysis of the speeches both from British and American leaders. His study shows that British politicians intend to pick up an underlying metaphorical proposition POLITICS IS RELITION to express their 'ethical values', and that such a conceptual shift from 'religious belief' to 'secular domain' results from the decline in attendance at formal religious services. He finds that apart from RELIGION metaphors, CONFLICT, BUILDING and JOURNEY metaphors are employed in the manifesto of British Party, and LIGHT, CONFLICT, JOURNEY, PHYSICAL ENVIRONMENT and BODY PARTS metaphors are used in US presidential speeches.

Metaphorical World Politics, edited by Beer and Landtsheer (2004), brings together a fascinating collection of articles that illuminates the multiple roles of metaphors in framing problems, prescribing solutions, and persuading others to support the decisions of political leaders regarding issues of democracy, national security and political economy. They argue that language and metaphor are important parts of international political reality and consider how metaphors may help to energize and structure international political thoughts and actions.

In *Political Metaphor Analysis*, Musolff (2016) focuses on the discussion of four major political metaphors that have been much debated publicly with a data-driven approach, namely, the depiction of politics and political entities in terms of war, family, body and person. In discussing these metaphors, he also talks about general issues of how figurative language is conceptually organized and how it is actually interpreted by real-life users rather than by introspectively "intuiting" linguists or by informants in artificially concocted and controlled experiments. These issues are considered not for their own sake, but for shedding light on political metaphor as an object of study for a critical linguistic enquiry that aims to understand real discourses as they are conducted, not as they should be according to a special theoretical or ideological framework.

While in China, Wang (2000) proposes that semantic research is not a patent of western scholars. Ever since ancient times in China, metaphors have been employed in such areas as state affairs, administration, counseling and debate.

Li (2000) lists the features of political metaphor in Russian newspaper writing, such as concentricity and expansion, popularity, death and revival of vividness which are closely related to the principles of construction of newspaper writing, that is, the stylization and vividness of language. She also argues that political metaphor is a figure of speech unique to newspaper writing. It is one of the important ways in which newspaper writing realizes its functions.

Zhu (2007) analyzes metaphors in relation to diseases, communications, climate, wars and kinship systems to demonstrate the cognitive relations between metaphor and politics on the basis of English and German. The commonalties and idiosyncrasies of political metaphor in different languages are also examined in his research from the perspective of cognitive linguistics.

Based on the analysis and explanation of both Chinese and English political metaphors, Cao (2008) identifies various stylistic functions of political metaphors, including interpreting function, expressing function, extending function and social function. These stylistic functions demonstrate the important role of metaphors in people's cognitive process.

Chen and Liu (2009) conduct a systematic research on the relationship between political metaphors and metaphorical concepts. They find that political metaphors are very popular among the American politicians because of their defining, persuading and information-processing functions. Moreover, the politicians use different metaphors: SPORTS and WAR metaphors are often used for their persuasive power and when dealing with the home and foreign political affairs, the politicians always resort to FAMILY, NEIGHBORHOOD and LEADERSHIP metaphors.

Through a diachronic analysis of the metaphors in the editorials extracted from People's Daily over the last three decades (1978 – 2007), Huang and Wu (2009) explore how the Communist Party of China has structured and restructured the composition of the conceptual metaphor for its updated use to manifest its leadership philosophy and guide the people effectively in constructing the modernization. They find that during the past thirty years the proportions of JOURNEY, CONSTRUCTION and PLANT metaphors kept stable, while those of WAR, NAVIGATION and FAMILY metaphors changed.

Through an analysis of the speech over the Libya War delivered by President Barack Obama at the National Defense University in Washington on March 28th, 2011, He (2011) explores the construction function of ideology in conceptual metaphor from the perspective of the frame theory. She argues that presupposition, foregrounding and creation of political myth are three ways for metaphor to realize the ideological construction. She then explains that metaphor building and metaphor use are conditioned by political power and political aim.

Wu and Pang (2011) have reported on a corpus-based study of metaphors in one major form of political discourse, namely, the presidential radio address. Taking CDA theory as the framework and with the help of 'Corpus for Specific Research of English', the study conducts a critical metaphorical analysis of the eight-year-long radio addresses delivered by the former President of the United States, George W. Bush, which aims to explore the types of conceptual metaphors used in Bush's justification of the Iraq War, as well as the persuasiveness of metaphors and the related discourse strategies. It is revealed that three major types of metaphors of conflict, illness and religion are used, in which metaphors play a significant role in stirring and evoking the audience's emotion. The use of metaphors also helps to rationalize and justify the speaker's course of action and his personal intention, so as to achieve the intended communicative goals.

Through a diachronic study of metaphors in *People's Daily*, Wang and Yang (2012) explore the function of different metaphors in the data from the perspective of cognition and discusses over the relation between the political metaphors and the political climate of a country.

Wang (2014) explores the frames and metaphors that the US government lives by from the cognitive perspective. He argues that it is vital to focus on the frames and metaphors behind the expressions of facts rather than facts themselves within the framework of second-generation cognitive science. After selecting the political discourses given by Republicans and Democrats concerning American foreign policies, economy, medical care and immigration, he then analyzes their respective frames and metaphors. It is revealed that the major frames and metaphors behind the discourses of the US government are: Nation is the Family; The Governing Individual is the Parent; Those Governed are Family Members; The Republic Party is Strict Father; The Democratic Party is a Nurturant Parent. The struggle between the two parties is characterized by framing and reframing of the same issues through different wordings. Both of them try their best to achieve conceptual manipulation by linking the expressions of the policies with their own morality through framing. It is the frames and metaphors that determine the acceptance of their policies by the public.

With an analysis in terms of metaphorical construction theory of George W. Bush's and Barack Obama's Medical Insurance Speeches, Liang and Wang (2015) find that differences in surface structure express the two Parties' different ideas of government while the deep structure mainly involves Bush's constructions of stimulating consumption, business and personal responsibility and Obama's constructions of price control and adjustment, social welfare and personal participation. Their study also shows that compared with Bush's speech of medical insurance, Obama's bill offers a more reasonable control of increase of expenditure of medical insurance. The construction of social welfare and stability in his speech makes it easier to realize the aim of expanding the coverage of medical insurance and the construction of personal participation assures a relatively high degree of acceptability.

Wu (2016) explores the persuasion mechanism and perception process of political metaphor and reaches the following conclusions: political metaphors enable people to make sense of political world by drawing from previous knowledge and experience in nonpolitical domains; political metaphors are aimed at transforming people's understanding into their attitudes and are thereby constitutive and persuasive; political metaphors' persuasion is based on the fact that they are at once emotional and rational, entailing a naming power; In metaphorical reasoning, political metaphor, by activating people's such perception processes as concept conventionality, structure mapping, and perception closure, and mainly taking advantage of such traits as selectivity, constancy, and wholeness of those processes, perform a function of facilitating and obstructing understanding at the same time, as well as legitimizing one idea while delegitimizing another.

Through the analysis of the conceptual metaphor, surface and deep frames in Bush's and Obama's environmental protection speeches within the framework of CMT and Framing Theory, Wang and Zhang (2017) find that similar metaphors, such as JOURNEY and STAGE, were both used in Bush's and Obama's speeches, with the former focusing more on frames of UNILATERAL DIPLOMACY and ECONOMIC INTERESTS

FIRST and the latter focusing more on MULTILATERAL DIPLOMACY, ECONOMY AND ENVIRONMENTAL PROTECTION BEING EQUALLY IMPROTANT. They then summarize the Metaphorical Framing Model of major American issues like environmental protection as morality, basic principles, conceptual metaphors and deep frames, metaphorical expressions and surface frames, inference, narrative role from the perspective of construction.

Chapter 3 Methodology

In this chapter I begin with a detailed description of the research methodology and data collection. Then I present the research procedure with CMA and the way we deal with the data in the corpus, including contextual analysis, metaphor identification, metaphor explanation and metaphor interpretation.

3.1 Research methodology and data collection

I am fully convinced that quantitative approach and qualitative approach stand in a dialectical complementation and thus work together unproblematically, and that both are essential for the investigation of metaphor. The methodology adopted in this book, therefore, is an integration of these two analyses. While a qualitative analysis is mainly concerned with the identification of metaphors and the description of general trends in the first place, then a quantitative analysis allows us to quantify the metaphorical language use in the corpus and estimate the extent to which metaphorically used words have become conventionalized – to answer questions like how common are metaphorical languages in political discourse? or which metaphor forms are most common?

Without quantitative analysis, we would not be able to demonstrate whether the use of a metaphor was novel or conventional since these notions depend on quantitative findings as to what is normal in language use. Qualitative analysis is also necessary to interpret the pragmatic role of metaphors as to whether they communicate a positive or a negative evaluation (Charteris-Black, 2004: 32 – 4).

For this reason, my suggestion here would be that a corpus-based approach into metaphor works best when both quantitative and qualitative analyses are involved and adopted in the corpus. Based on the procedure of identification, categorization and comparative analysis of the conceptual metaphors in the public speeches by former US President Barack Obama and former Chinese President Hu Jintao, the present study discusses the similarities and differences between the conceptual metaphors in the two data.

The approach adopted in this book is introduced with reference to a number of real and concrete examples and the collected data potentially ensures the "comparability" within different cultural background; that is, the data are restricted to the similar situation constraints, including discourse participant, occasion, genre, field and mode. Specifically, the data are collected from five public speeches by former US President Barack Obama (see http//:*www. whitehouse. gov* for the full texts) and five public speeches by former Chinese President Hu Jintao (see http//:*www. cctv. com* for full texts) respectively. To make a comparative analysis, the identified conceptual metaphors in the two languages are to be divided into two major categories: the same or similar conceptual metaphors and the different conceptual metaphors. Additionally, the linguistic entity, frequency and case number of each conceptual metaphor will be presented as well. Table 1 offers a picture of the data.

Table 1 Speeches from two leaders

Speeches	Subject
胡锦涛在国庆60周年大会上发表的重要讲话(2009.10.1) Hu Jintao's Speech on the 60th Anniversary of the National Day (Oct 1, 2009)	Address on National Independence
Barack Obama's Remarks at Independence Day Celebration (July 4, 2010)	
胡锦涛在早稻田大学的演讲(2008.5.8) Hu Jintao's Speech in Waseda University (May 8, 2008)	Address in University
Barack Obama's Speech in Fudan University (Nov 16, 2009)	
胡锦涛在四川召开的抗震救灾工作会议上的讲话(2008.5.17) Hu Jintao's Address on Earthquake Resistance and Disaster Relief in Sichuan Province (May 17, 2008)	Address on Earthquake Resistance and Disaster Relief
Barack Obama's Remarks on Recovery Efforts in Haiti (Jan 14, 2010)	
胡锦涛在全国政协新年茶话会上的讲话(2010.1.1) Hu Jintao's Speech on the CPPCC New Year Tea Party (Jan 1, 2010)	New Year Greetings
Barack Obama's Remarks on Thanksgiving (Nov 26, 2009)	
胡锦涛在澳门特别行政区第三届政府就职典礼上的讲话(2009.12.20) Hu Jintao's Speech on the Inaugural Ceremony of the 3th Government in Macao Special Administrative Region (Dec 20, 2009)	Inaugural Address
Barack Obama's Inaugural Address (Jan 20, 2009)	

Table 1 shows that the data, collected from public speeches by former US President Barack Obama and former Chinese President Hu Jintao, mainly cover social and political issues, such as national independence, earthquake resistance and disaster relief and inaugural address. In the course of the book, I have considered a range of critical issues in data collection and metaphor identification beforehand, specifically, with respect to data search, representativeness, balance and indirectness, such that I would be able to guarantee the validity and reliability of this study. The quantitative approach is employed in data collection while qualitative approach is used in data analysis. With a comparative analysis of the conceptual metaphors identified in the data, I then analyze and discuss the similarities and differences between the conceptual metaphors based on the frequency, distribution and the usage of the data.

3.2 Research procedure

In this section, I will introduce what Charteris-Black (2004) describes as CMA and explain in more detail why CMA could contribute to answering the fundamental questions in this book. According to him, CMA aims to identify which metaphors are chosen in such persuasive genres as political speeches or press reports and attempts to explain why these metaphors are chosen, with reference to the interaction between an orator's purposes and a specific set of speech circumstances. In a political context, CMA involves demonstrating how metaphors are used systematically to create political myths and discourses of legitimization and delegitimization that give rise to ideologies and world views (Charteris-Black, 2014: 174). Figure 1 provides an overview of four principal stages of CMA.

3.2.1 Contextual analysis

The first stage of CMA is to develop research questions about metaphor that should emerge from an awareness of its potential for rhetoric impact in social and political contexts. CMA identifies and investigates metaphors that are employed systematically to represent vulnerable social groups in a negative way, or to represent policies as being in the interests of all (ibid: 174). Questions might be in this study, for instance, "What metaphors are selected by Chinese president and American president respectively to motivate, inspire and even evoke strong e-

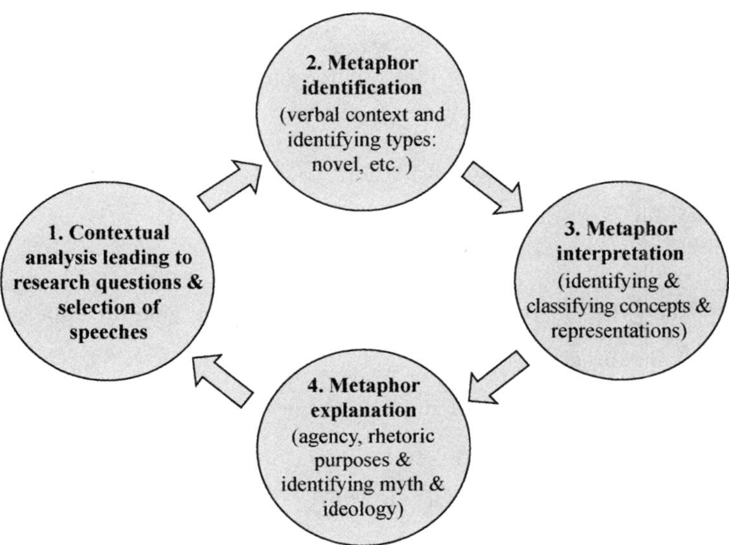

Figure 1 Principle stages of critical metaphor analysis

motional responses among people in his nation?" Decisions will be taken regarding the speaker, the time period, the number of texts and so on – all of which determine the dataset to be examined (ibid: 174).

3.2.2 Metaphor identification

Metaphor identification is a presupposition of metaphor studies at any time in history. According to Charteris-Black (2004: 35 – 7), metaphor identification has two stages: the first stage requires a close reading of a sample of texts with the aim of identifying candidate metaphors. These candidates are then examined with reference to the linguistic, pragmatic and cognitive criteria for the definition of metaphor. We will further make sure that these candidate metaphors are the presence of incongruity or semantic tension resulting from a transfer in domain use. In other words, whatever sense a word or phrase originally had, a metaphor is formed when this word or phrase is used in a new context with a different sense that creates some type of semantic tension or continuity (Charteris-Black, 2014: 177). This standard is basically consistent with what Pragglejaz[①] Group (2007) describes as 'Metaphor Identification Procedure (MIP)'.

- Read the entire text-discourse to establish a general understanding of the meaning.
- Determine the lexical units in the text-discourse

(a) For each lexical unit in the text, establish its meaning in context, that is, how it applies to an entity, relation, or attribute in the situation evoked by the text (contextual meaning). Take into account what comes before and after the lexical unit.

(b) For each lexical unit, determine if it has a more basic contemporary meaning in other contexts than the one in the given context. For our purposes, basic meanings tend to be

—More concrete (what they evoke is easier to imagine, see, hear, feel, smell, and taste);

—Related to bodily action;

—More precise (as opposed to vague);

—Historically older;

Basic meanings are not necessarily the most frequent meanings of the lexical unit.

(c) If the lexical unit has a more basic current-contemporary meaning in other contexts than the given context, decide whether the

① The name Pragglejaz is formed by the initials of the first names of the ten scholars of the group: Peter Crisp, Raymond Gibbs, Alan Cienki, Gerard Steen, Graham Low, Lynne Cameron, Elena Semino, Joseph Grady, Alice Deignan and Zoltán Kövecses.

contextual meaning contrasts with the basic meaning but can be understood in comparison with it.

- If yes, mark the lexical unit as metaphorical.

(Pragglejaz Group, 2007: 3)

It can therefore be seen that with MIP a lexical unit could be marked as metaphorical if it has a more basic current-contemporary meaning in other contexts than the given context, and the contextual meaning contrasts with the basic meaning but can be understood in comparison with the basic meaning. Metaphors in political rhetoric typically occur in phrases, or collocations, rather than separate words, and for this reason, the division line between these two methods lies on the fact that whether the unit of measurement should be the phrase or the word (Charteris-Black, 2014: 176). Those that do not fall within the criterion will be excluded from further analysis. Qualified words with metaphorical senses are then categorized as metaphor keywords and it is possible to measure the presence of such keywords quantitatively in the corpus. The second stage is a further qualitative analysis in which corpus contexts are examined to determine whether each use of a keyword is metaphorical or not.

Evidence from general corpus of language provides a robust method for critical metaphor analysis and is helpful in establishing the different types of metaphor we may wish to count, especially when building on the psycholinguistic approach (ibid: 178).

- Novel metaphors (usually processed by comparison) can evoke empathetic responses and contribute to powerful, heroic narratives.
- Entrenched metaphors (usually processed by categorization) can

reveal the ideology behind the framing of issues in a certain way.

• Conventional metaphors (processing shifts between comparison and categorization, depending on context) can reveal such grammar of metaphor in large corpus as the collocates, part of speech and semantic prosody around metaphorical expressions.

However, identification and classification of metaphors is necessarily a slow and at times a laborious process, preferably undertaken by more than one analysts to ensure the reliability of the findings. A robust method is to analyze speeches in five phases, preferably on different days, as summarized in Figure 2 (ibid: 179 – 180).

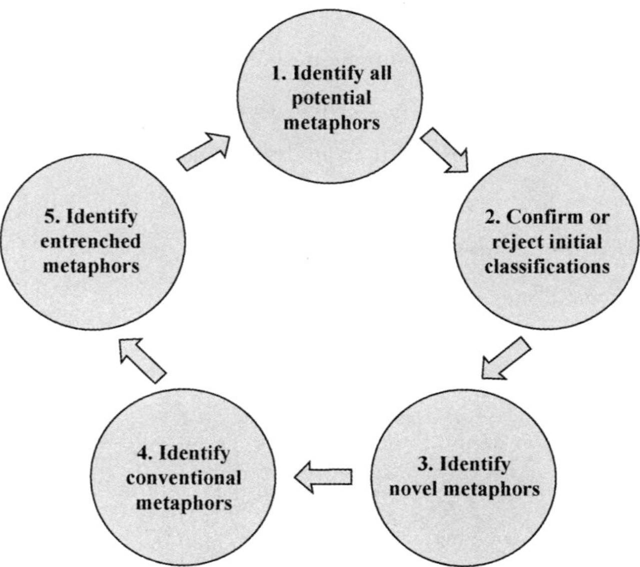

Figure 2 Method for critical metaphor analysis

• Identify all potential metaphors by working through a text with a marker pen; initially, all candidate metaphors can be identified.

• Confirm or reject initial decisions – drawing on dictionaries to establish whether there is more basic sense of a word, and corpora to identify whether the word is usually metaphorical; and decisions taken with regard to the type of metaphor.

• From the list in stage two, identify novel 'metaphors', that is, words and phrases that are likely to be processed by comparison. These may be indicated in the title of a speech. They are likely to be processed by comparison in short-term memory and are influential in contributing to audience response.

• Identify conventional metaphors – the ones that a corpus shows have become a pattern such as 'beacon of hope', and where these words are metaphors between 5 and 50 occurrences in a sample of 100 lines.

• Identify entrenched metaphors – these might have been completely invisible in the first phrase because they have become naturalized. They will occur in over half of the lines in a sample of 100.

3.2.3 Metaphor interpretation

Metaphor interpretation first involves establishing a relationship between metaphors and the cognitive and pragmatic factors that determine them. This stage includes the identification of conceptual metaphors, and where feasible, conceptual keys (Charteris-Black, 2004: 37 – 8). This is deciding how metaphors are to be classified, organized and arranged. Classification of metaphors on the basis of the literal meaning of words is known as organizing by source domain, whereas classification on the basis of what metaphors refer to in context is called organizing by target domain. What follows involves working out the particular meanings, representations and evaluations conveyed by the speaker – typically deciding whether these metaphors are positive or negative (Charteris-Black, 2014: 175 – 176).

3.2.4 Metaphor explanation

Explanation of metaphors involves identifying the social agency that is involved in their production and their social role in persuasion (Charteris-Black, 2004: 39), which requires judging whether and how metaphors influenced an audience, how they interacted with other features and their persuasive role in forming, consolidating or changing opinions, ideas and beliefs (Charteris-Black, 2014: 176). In a sense, it is identifying the discourse functions of metaphors that permits us to establish their ideological and rhetorical motivation. Evidence for ideological and rhetorical motivation comes from the corpus in which metaphors occur rather than from the intuition of the analyst (Charteris-Black, 2004: 39).

Chapter 4 Data Description and Analysis

The precondition of conducting a comparative analysis of conceptual metaphors in English and Chinese data is the identification of the metaphorically used words in the political languages and then the formulation of the corresponding conceptual metaphors. Thus, a comparative analysis of conceptual metaphors found in the data may assist us exploring the similarities and differences between these metaphors and distilling the underlying factors behind them.

4.1 Conceptual metaphors in English data

In President Barack Obama's data, it can be found that abstract thoughts and concepts in the target domains are commonly constructed and characterized in terms of the habitual and routine bodily and social patterns that American people experience and what they learn of the experience of others. These patterns of experience in the political domain that tend to be constructed metaphorically are numerous and varied, and are closely related to people's daily functioning, which at least include the following:

- The current state of affairs, and particularly the problems that need to be solved;
- Causes and solutions to problem;
- Plans and policies;
- Future states of affairs, including positive scenarios (resulting from one's policies), and negative scenarios (resulting from opponents' policies);
- Various types of participants and entities in the political domains (including private citizens, parties, organizations, institutions, states);
- The 'in-group' (oneself, one's party, government, social group, nation or race), as opposed to the 'out-group' (other individuals, other parties, social groups, nations or races);
- Politics and political action themselves.

(Semino, 2008: 91)

While any area of experience can potentially function as metaphorical source domain in politics, some source domains have been found to be particularly dominant in the studies of American presidential political speeches, which include the domain of JOURNEY, HUMAN, BUILDING, DRAMA, FAMILY and RELIGION. In what follows, these source domains in English data are to be described and analyzed in more detail.

4.1.1 JOURNEY metaphor

JOURNEY metaphors were originally introduced into cognitive metaphor study by Lakoff and Johnson (1980: 44 - 5) who initially proposed the metaphor LOVE IS A JOURNEY to account for the linguistic expressions such as *we're just spinning our wheels*; *our marriage is on the rocks*; *this relationship is a dead-end street etc.* and this was later developed into a more general metaphor LIFE IS A JOURNEY (Lakoff & Turner 1989: 10). They traced the origin of this metaphor in the Judeo-Christian tradition through alternative paths of righteousness and evil ways (ibid: 10). In these representations, a journey is taken as a prototype purposeful activity involving movement in physical space from a starting point to a destination (Charteris-Black 2004: 74). This metaphor was later reformulated into PURPOSEFUL ACTIVITY IS TRAVELLING ALONG A PATH TOWARD A DESTINATION (Lakoff 1993). Charteris-Black (2011: 74) suggests that social purposes can be viewed as destination just as much as individual ones. Evidence for this idea can be found in metaphoric uses of 'step', 'burden', 'forward' and so on.

Therefore, JOURNEY metaphors can be traced back to the PATH image schema, which is based in our physical experience of motion in space (Semino, 2008: 92). Its required component elements include a starting point and a destination connected by a path and entities that move along the path. Optional elements are, however, equally important in political discourse, which include mode of travel, guides, companions, etc (Charteris-Black, 2011: 66). The PATH image schema provides a way of metaphorically constructing goals as destinations, ways of reaching goals as movement forwards, problems as obstacles to movement, and success or failure as reaching, or failing to reach, a destination (Semino, 2008: 92).

Political discourse is the product of high abstraction and conceptualization of our human mind where the concrete conceptual domains with a highly organized structure that are commonly mapped onto the relatively abstract conceptual domains that do not possess systematic structures. In English data, it is found that 'journey' can be identified as a source domain in that it is grounded in human bodily experience. Journey involves travelers, predetermined paths, modes of travel, starting point and end point; the purpose of travelers is to march towards a destination with vehicles or routes. Reaching the destination, however, is not an easy task as there are impediments, landmarks and crossroads that block progress on the way.

Charteris-Black (2011: 45) argues that the JOURNEY metaphor provides a mental representation that allows the various aspects of political experience to be understood and expressed via embodied experience of movement. The 'journey' schema is rhetorically attractive to politicians and leaders because it can be turned into a whole scenario when they represent themselves as 'guide', their policies as 'map' and their supporters as 'fellow travelling companion'. All of these entailments of the source domain contribute to the trust the politicians seek to establish.

In JOURNEY metaphors, the purposes of politicians' actions are conceptualized as the destinations of the travelers with an implication that they want to attain a predetermined end. Normally, JOURNEY metaphors positively evaluate policies because the ends are socially valued ones though there are hardships that may prevent or hinder the achievement of a goal. Therefore, JOURNEY metaphor implies that achieving worthwhile goals can be represented by the conceptual metaphor PURPOSEFUL SOCIAL ACTIVITY IS TRAVELING ALONG A PATH TO A DESTINATION (Charteris-Black, 2004: 93). The following examples are partial realization of this conceptual metaphor.

(1) And just as I'm impressed by these signs of China's **journey** to the 21st century, I'm eager to see those ancient places that speak to us from China's distant past.

(Barack Obama's Speech in Fudan University)

(2) In reaffirming the greatness of our nation, we understand that greatness is never a given. It must be earned. Our **journey** has never been one of **short-cuts** or settling for less. It has not been the **path** for the faint-hearted, for those that prefer leisure over work, or seek only the pleasures of riches and fame.

(Barack Obama's Inaugural Address)

(3) Of course, this small opening was followed by the achievement of the Shanghai Communique, and the eventual establishment of formal relations between the United States and China in 1979. And in three decades, just look at **how far** we have come.

(Barack Obama's Speech in Fudan University)

(4) So let this be the next **step** in the steady pursuit of cooperation that will serve our nations, and the world. And if there's one thing that we can take from today's dialogue, I hope that it is a commitment to continue this dialogue **going forward**.

(Barack Obama's Speech in Fudan University)

The development of a nation is being conceptualized as a person walking towards the predetermined goal or destination. However, it takes time to endure the endless suffering of going on journey in that there might be unexpected obstacles and different types of hazards that people may encounter while travelling – such as meeting a dead end or getting lost. Therefore, a traveler has to walk along the road with a right direction that it would be possible to reach the destination. In metaphorical terms, the optional elements are that her people should persist in their dreams, devoting themselves to the social interests as well as the personal development.

Although JOURNEY metaphor may imply either positive evaluations (step, go forward) or negative ones (hardship, tolerate), it still presents a strong positive orientation even when the negative aspects of a journey are highlighted by the metaphor – such as endure the hardships – the effort and confidence that are necessary to achieve anything is evaluated as worthwhile (ibid: 93). Consider the following examples,

(5) Rather, it has been the risk-takers, the doers, the makers of things – some celebrated, but more often men and women obscure in their labor – who have carried us up the **long**, **rugged path** towards prosperity and freedom.

(Barack Obama's Inaugural Address)

(6) Finally, I want to speak directly to the people of Haiti. Few in the world have **endured** the **hardships** that you have known. Long before this tragedy, daily life itself was often a bitter struggle.

(Barack Obama's Remarks on Recovery Efforts in Haiti)

(7) Now, there are some who question the scale of our ambitions, who suggest that our system cannot **tolerate** too many big plans.

(Barack Obama's Inaugural Address)

(8) A different kind of connection was made nearly 40 years ago when the **frost** between our countries began to **thaw** through the simple game of table tennis.

(Barack Obama's Speech in Fudan University)

Obviously, the frustration and hardships that American people experienced are positively evaluated with the use of metaphor just because of the value of common goal shared among people in this nation. One of the shared understandings is that overcoming an obstacle or a barrier that hinders movement along the road is justified because the destination itself is valued. These metaphors also highlight the need for patience since it will take time and efforts to reach a destination.

This is rhetorically effective because it implies a need for patience and guards against expectations of instant benefits from the government policies, and that, at times, society will need to suffer in order to achieve goals. It also implies that hardships are to be tolerated because these goals are worthwhile (ibid: 93). In this respect, JOURNEY metaphors encourage people to bear short-term suffering in order to gain worthwhile long-term objectives.

Moreover, a traveler needs to make a choice among different paths that can be to different places along the journey since there is no alternative to the predetermined destination. In political discourse, social goals proposed by the government are commonly conceptualized as destinations in the travelers' minds, which include long-term goals and short-term ones. In American presidential speeches, the destinations depicted by the leaders usually refer to gaining freedom, democracy and liberty. Therefore, the metaphorical concept COMMON PURPOSES ARE DESTINATIONS is employed in English data and this can be reflected in the following examples.

(9) Their memories are short, for they have forgotten what this country has already done, what free men and women can **achieve** when imagination is joined to **common purpose**, and ne-

cessity to courage.

(Barack Obama's Inaugural Address)

(10) This is a **common American impulse** – **the desire** to **reach** for new horizons, and to forge new partnerships that are mutually beneficial.

(Barack Obama's Speech in Fudan University)

(11) They argue that our health care system is fine the way it is and that a clean energy economy can wait. They say we are trying to do too much, that we are moving too quickly, and that we all ought to just take a deep breath and scale back our **goals**.

(Barack Obama's Remarks on Thanksgiving)

(12) Rather, it has been the risk-takers, the doers, the makers of things – some celebrated, but more often men and women obscure in their labor – who have carried us up the long, rugged path **towards** prosperity and freedom.

(Barack Obama's Inaugural Address)

(13) The success of our economy has always depended not just on the size of our gross domestic product, but on the **reach** of our prosperity, on the ability to extend opportunity to every willing heart – not out of charity, but because it is the **surest route** to our **common good**.

(Barack Obama's Inaugural Address)

It is usually the knowledge that travelers may turn to a guide for the right way towards the desirable destination when encountering a dead end or even getting lost on a journey. Within CMT, the God is often represented as a guide and it is only the guide who knows the destination in American culture; as her people feel miserable and lose confidence overcoming the obstruction on their own, the God always gives them power and guide them to the right direction. The conceptual metaphor FAITH IS GUIDE therefore can be identified in American political speeches in the following examples.

(14) The **God-given promise** that all are equal, all are free, and all deserve a chance to pursue their full measure of happiness.

(Barack Obama's Inaugural Address)

(15) But those **values** upon which our success depends - honesty and hard work, courage and fair play, tolerance and curiosity, loyalty and patriotism - these things are old. These things are true.

(Barack Obama's Inaugural address)

(16) That's the **spirit** we must summon as we make a new beginning for our nation.

(Barack Obama's Remarks on thanks giving)

(17) The United States, by comparison, is a young nation, whose culture is determined by so many different immigrants who have come to our shores, and by the founding documents that **guide** our democracy.

(Barack Obama's speech in Fudan University)

4.1.2 HUMAN metaphor

Personification is a particularly important and pervasive type of metaphor, since it involves the use of our experience and knowledge of human beings as source domain (Semino, 2008: 101). Under CMT view, personification is primarily treated as a type of ontological metaphor whereby abstract and non-human entities are described in terms of human motivations, characteristics and activities. Personification, as a general category, covers a wide range of conceptual metaphors, each picking out different aspects of a person or ways of looking at a person (Lakoff & Johnson, 1980: 33 – 4).

It can therefore be argued that 'person' should be seen as the source domain. As human beings, we can best understand other things in our own terms. Personification permits us to use our knowledge about ourselves to maximal effect, to use insights about ourselves to help us comprehend such things as forces of nature, common events, abstract concepts, and inanimate objects (Lakoff & Turner, 1989: 72). In political discourse, personification is widely used, particularly in relation to entities and institutions such as nation states (Semino, 2008: 101). Personification is persuasive because it evokes our attitudes, feelings and beliefs about people and applies them to our attitudes, feelings and beliefs about abstract political entities and therefore is a way of heightening the emotional appeal (Charteris-Black, 2011: 61).

Just as the former US President Franklin D. Roosevelt says in his third inaugural address in January 1941, "A nation, like a person, has a body – a body that must be fed and clothed and housed, invigorated and rested, in a manner that measures up to the objectives of our time; A nation, like a person, has a mind – a mind that must be kept informed and alert, that must know itself, that understands the hopes and the needs of its neighbors – all the other nations that live within the narrowing circle of the world; A nation, like a person, has something deeper, something more permanent, something larger than the sum of all its parts."

We are then suggesting that the personification of countries and nations can be represented in terms of relatively simple and concrete human scenarios, such as human motivations, goals, actions, and characteristics. In extract (18), 'America' is represented as the agent of action referred to by the verb 'stand'. Since the action is prototypically associated with human beings, we may suggest that the referent of America is personified, namely, represented as individual human agent. Thus, In English data, the following examples can be presumably motivated by the conceptual metaphor A NATION IS A PERSON.

(18) To the people of Haiti, we say clearly, and with conviction, you will not be forsaken; you will not be forgotten. In this, your hours of greatest need, America **stands** with you.

(Barack Obama's Remarks on Recovery Efforts in Haiti)

(19) Today, we are called to remember not only the day our country was **born** – we are also called to remember the indomitable spirit of the first American citizens who made that day possible.

(Barack Obama's Remarks on National Independence)

(20) And the United States has **seen** our economy grow along with the standard of living enjoyed by our people, while bringing the Cold War to a successful conclusion.

(Barack Obama's Speech in Fudan University)

(21) most importantly, the **compassion** of our country.

(Barack Obama's Remarks on Recovery Efforts in Haiti)

Lakoff (2003) argues that HUMAN metaphor is pervasive, powerful, and part of an elaborate metaphor system. It is part of an International Community metaphor, in which there are friendly nations, hostile nations, rogue states, and so on. This metaphor comes with a notion of the national interest: Just as it is in the interest of a person to be healthy and strong, so it is in the interest of a Nation-Person to be economically healthy and militarily strong.

The fact is that a nation coexists with many others in the international relations community within the conceptual metaphor A NATION IS A PERSON, entailing that the relationship between different countries and nations, like that among human beings, can be strengthened and enhanced on the basis of, for instance, mutual respect, trust, understanding and cooperation, that a nation could "partner" with others if she realizes that it is of great importance to establish the bilateral relationship and boost the tie. From the perspective of CMT, we talk about and, potentially, reason about that relationship between different nations and countries in terms of personified concepts based on the conceptual metaphor OTHER COUNTRIES ARE PARTNERS AND COMPANIONS. Consider the following examples,

(22) However, America's **ties** to this city – and to this country – stretch back further, to the earliest days of America's independence.

(Barack Obama's Speech in Fudan University)

(23) In 1979, the political **cooperation** between the United States and China was rooted largely in our shared rivalry with the Soviet Union.

(Barack Obama's Speech in Fudan University)

(24) We will **partner** with other nations and organizations.

(Barack Obama's Remarks on Recovery Efforts)

(25) We stand in solidarity with our **neighbors** to the south, knowing that but for the grace of God, there we go.

(Barack Obama's Remarks on Recovery Efforts)

4.1.3 BUILDING metaphor

BUILDING metaphor was initially identified in Lakoff and Johnson's book *Metaphors We Live By* (1980) to structure the concept of 'theory'. This metaphor allows us to use expressions such as 'construct' and 'foundation' from one domain (building) to talk, about and potentially, reason about the corresponding concepts in the metaphorically defined domain (theory). In normal case, the schematic framework for our knowledge of a good building is that it should be based on a solid foundation or structure with perfectly firm stuff, or it collapses and even leads to disastrous consequences. Technically, the entities in the category of a nation's development are commonly being conceptualized as those in the category of the construction of a building in American presidential speeches.

Metaphors from the source domain of building usually carry a strong positive orientation because they express aspiration towards desirable social goals. Charteris-Black (2004: 71) then suggests that BUILDING metaphors are motivated by a conceptual metaphor SOCIETY IS BUILDING and invariably convey a positive evaluation because a valued outcome requires social cooperation between government and the people. Social goals are conceptualized as needing patience and effort because instant outcomes are not expected. The uses of such metaphorical concepts are therefore evident in the formulation of the conceptual metaphors DEVELOPING A COUNTRY IS CREATING A BUILDING and AMERICAN PEOPLE ARE BUILDERS, which are used to represent a strong and powerful economy. Consider the following examples,

(26) It is what led generations of American workers to **build** an industrial economy unrivalled around the world.

(Barack Obama's Inaugural Address)

(27) For the sake of our economy and our children, we must **build** on the historic bill passed by the House of Representatives.

(Barack Obama's Inaugural Address)

(28) So we've made progress. But we cannot rest – and my administration will not rest – until we have revived this economy and **rebuilt** it stronger than before.

(Barack Obama's Remarks on Recovery Efforts in Haiti)

(29) In addition to your growing economy, we admire China's extraordinary commitment to science and research – a commitment borne out in everything from the infrastructure you **build** to the technology you use.

(Barack Obama's Speech in Fudan University)

BUILDING metaphors are, typically, examples of reification. For example – when we 'build' collocates with abstract goals such as trust and respect – as in the following.

(30) We have seen what is possible when we **build upon** our mutual interests, and engage on the basis of mutual respect.

(Barack Obama's Speech in Fudan University)

4.1.4 DRAMA metaphor

Drama has a number of characteristics that appear to be valuable to the metaphor when applied to politics. It is structured, designed in what it shows, artful, purposeful, and goal-oriented. This can make politics seem ordered, skillful, focused, purposeful, and meaningful on the one hand, or determined, superficial, histrionic, deceptive, instrumental, and manipulative on the other (Fitzgerald, 2015: 43).

The main elements included DRAMA metaphors are tragedy, scenario, actor, spectator, performance, role, and image. However, the key to DRAMA metaphor is spectatorship because what the metaphor allows users to do is to objectify what lies before their gaze in such a way as to make it seem to have the characteristics of a drama performed on a stage (ibid: 43). Thus, when politics is described as theater, a spectator is necessarily invoked not just because theater involves spectatorship but because metaphor users are spectators. Spectatorship is also invoked in recipients because metaphors prompt them to see a phenomenon differently. In the process, recipients are turned into spectators (ibid: 9).

It is the commonsense that the natural disaster may cause casualties and bring great losses to a country and that people from international community will show deep sorrow and sympathy for the bereaved family. Similarly, the natural disaster is commonly being conceptualized as a tragedy in the following sentences, with implication that American people even cry for the losses of Haiti, which is somewhat like a play or a tragedy for the sake of international humanitarian relief. Consider the following examples,

(31)... and looking for meaning in a **tragedy** that seems so blind and random.

(Barack Obama's Remarks on Recovery Efforts in Haiti)

(32) The reason I'm proud to be here with him and Governor

and Senator is because in spite of the terrible **tragedy** their spirits are high.

(Barack Obama's Remarks on Recovery Efforts in Haiti)

It is suggested that US government has commonly treated herself as an actor or a performer on the world stage, with the rest of the world as spectators. Therefore, in American presidential speeches, it is not surprising that the government and her citizens are often being conceptualized as actors or performers, playing a crucial role on the stage. Generally speaking, if every performer does his part well on the stage, the drama, then, could turn to be a great success. The uses of the metaphorically expressions such as 'playing a crucial role' and 'do its part' reveal the mapping from the concrete domain of 'performer' to the abstract domain of 'federal government'. The following sentences are therefore the partial linguistic realizations of the conceptual metaphor GOVERNMENT IS AN ACTOR.

(33) State and local governments **performed** skillfully under the worst conditions.

(Barack Obama's Remarks on Recovery Efforts in Haiti)

(34) Federal government is **playing** a crucial role in helping the people of the devastated areas to recover.

(Obama's Remarks on Recovery Efforts in Haiti)

(35) I also met relief and rescue workers who are **performing** heroically in difficult circumstances.

(Barack Obama's Remarks on Recovery Efforts in Haiti)

(36) And the federal government will do its **part**.

(Barack Obama's Remarks on Recovery Efforts in Haiti)

It can be found that social activities can be represented as dramas that are able to depict the strength of American economy and even the whole picture of the nation. Specifically, in American political language, the federal government and citizens that do their part well in these social activities are being conceptualized as actors who perform skillfully on the stage in order to present an excellent show or a play. We could therefore formulate the conceptual metaphor SOCIAL ACTIVITY IS A DRAMA through the following examples.

(37) Our successful businesses **show** the strength of American commerce.

(Barack Obama's Remarks on Thanksgiving)

(38) America **shows** that a society can be vast and varied.

(Barack Obama's Remarks on Thanksgiving)

(39) And we'll once more **show** the world that the worst adversities brim out the best in America.

(Barack Obama's Remarks on National Independence)

4.1.5 FAMILY metaphor

Lakoff (2004: 153 – 5) argues that Nation-as-Family metaphors exist as part of the standard conceptual repertoire in American politics, with the basic knowledge that the nation is a family, that the government is a parent and the citizens are the children. This metaphorical concept allows us to make sense of the nation potentially on the basis of what we know about family. In fact, part of human beings' conceptual systems, whether they are liberals, conservatives, or neither, is a common metaphorical conception of the Nation-as-Family, with the government, or head of state representing the nation, seen as an older male authority figure, typically as a father.

In American history, for example, George Washington was commonly conceptualized as "the founding father of his country", partly because he was the metaphorical "progenitor" who brought it into being and partly because he was seen as the ultimate legitimate head of state, which according to this metaphor is the head of the family, the father. A nation may be called either the "fatherland" or the "motherland" though with somewhat different implications. The following sentences are some of the linguistic reflection of this conceptual metaphor.

(40) Our **founding fathers**, faced with perils that we can scarcely imagine, drafted a charter to assure the rule of law and the rights of man – a charter expanded by the blood of generations.

(Barack Obama's Remarks on National Independence)

(41) At the moment when the outcome of our revolution was most in doubt, the **father** of our nation ordered these words to be read to the people.

(Barack Obama's Remarks on National Independence)

(42) And we say special thanks... for all those Americans who enrich the lives of **our communities** through acts of kindness, generosity and service.

(Barack Obama's Remarks on Thanksgiving)

This metaphor, however, does not clarify what kind of family the nation is and the ambiguity leads to two different models of family tradition, the STRICT FATHER model and the NURTURANT PARENT model.

The STRICT FATHER model takes the view that life is difficult and the world is fundamentally dangerous. As the traditional nuclear family, the father has primary responsibility for supporting and protecting the family as well as the authority to set overall family policy in a harsh world. In order to develop the independence of children, they should be rewarded when they do right and punished when they are wrong. The mother has the responsibility for the care of the house, raising the children, and upholding the father's authority (ibid: 65 – 6). As children, they are "governed" and "ruled" by their parents and told to be self-disciplined and independent in the family. They must respect and obey the parents' instructions.

However, NURTURANT PARENT model treats the world as less dangerous and more promising than the STRICT FATHER model, and emphasizes cooperation more than conflict and competition. The primal experience behind the NURTURANT PARENT model is one of being cared for and cared about, having one's desires for loving interactions met, living as happily as possible, and deriving meaning from mutual interaction and care (ibid: 108).

Lakoff (2004: 12) then argues that liberals and conservatives have very different moral systems, and that much of the political discourse of conservatives and liberals derives from their moral systems. Conservativism is based on a STRICT FATHER model, while liberalism is centered around a NURTURANT PARENT model. For example, Bush's administration represents "the strict father", and his job is to protect his family and teach his children right from wrong. In other words, this model seeks to impose her idea of order, rewarding and punishing accordingly, and otherwise seeking to make her citizens defend for themselves. However, we find that Obama's administration adopts both STRICT FATHER model and NURTURANT PARENT model and the conceptual metaphor GOVERNMENT IS A STRICT AND NURTURANT PARENT can be reflected in the following examples.

(43) So we've made progress. But we cannot rest – and **my administration** will **not rest** – until we have revived this economy and rebuilt it stronger than before.

(Barack Obama's Remarks on Recovery Efforts in Haiti)

(44) My **fellow** citizens: I stand here today humbled by the task before us, grateful for the trust you've bestowed, mindful of the sacrifices borne by our ancestors.

(Barack Obama's Remarks on Thanksgiving)

(45) **Government** should reflect the will of the people and respond to their wishes.

(Barack Obama's Remarks on National Independence)

4.1.6 RELIGIOUS metaphor

RELIGIOUS metaphors are found to be commonly used in American political context. Young (1993: 420) explains that religion was put to the most useful service it could perform for a crusading politician of the later twentieth century. It reduced to simple issues of personal morality highly complex questions of social and economic behavior. Charteris-Black (2004: 103 – 4) argues that religion has played an important part in the evolution of the USA and Christian evangelism has been an important source of inter-racial and inter-ethnic harmony. Religion serves as a source domain for invoking spiritual aspirations into the political domain and links the president with a commitment to Christian religious belief.

In addition, the systematic use of RELIGIOUS metaphor on the part of American politicians, in particular, may not just be an expression of religious belief, but also a strategic way of representing one's own identity as a potential leader, establishing common ground with some parts of the public and lack of common ground with others, and exploiting some of the emotional associations of religious images for rhetoric ends (semino, 2008: 104).

It is the cultural knowledge that religion is an indispensable part in western tradition where people believe in God and treat Bible as the spiritual support and basic doctrines for actions in life. Therefore, it comes as no surprise that in political speeches RELIGIOUS metaphors are significant and the concepts of religion are often employed by politicians to make the ideas more impelling and convincing. This can be manifested in JOURNEY metaphor in which the God is represented as the guide or map, with implications that God will always be there with American people even if when they are in dilemma and that America will get through hardships and difficulties with the guide of the God.

Thus, it can be seen that the cultural knowledge of religion provides some evidence for the conceptual metaphor POLITICS IS RELIGION. Consider the following examples,

(46) At these moments, America has carried on not simply because of the skill or **vision** of those in high office, but because we the people have remained **faithful** to the ideals of our forbearers, and true to our founding documents.

(Barack Obama's Inaugural Address)

(47) Your spirit has been unbroken and your **faith** has been

unwavering.

(Barack Obama's Remarks on Recovery Efforts in Haiti)

(48) For as much as government can do and must do, determination of the American people upon which it is ultimately the **faith** and this nation relies.

(Barack Obama's Inaugural Address)

(49) This is the meaning of our liberty and our **creed** – why men and women and children of every race and every **faith** can join in celebration across this magnificent mall, and why a man whose father less than sixty years ago might not have been served at a local restaurant can now stand before you to take a most **sacred oath**.

(Barack Obama's Inaugural Address)

(50) The God-given **promise** that all are equal, all are free, and all deserve a chance to pursue their full measure of happiness.

(Barack Obama's Inaugural Address)

The uses of words such as 'faith', 'vision', 'creed' and 'promise' in American politics are identified as metaphorical used words from the domain of religion.

As we know, an important objective for political leadership is to create an image that the politician is to be trusted because they have a plan for the future that is inherently good. In this respect, a very common choice of metaphor is that of 'vision', which also activates the religious idea of a visionary – or one who has supernatural powers to predict future (Charteris-Black, 2011: 183).

Faith, then, is commonly being conceptualized as a state of belief that can give American people power, confidence and hope, especially in times of hardships and frustration, while 'vision' is used to conceptualize political aspirations and objectives in the future.

4.2 Conceptual metaphors in Chinese data

In the former Chinese President Hu Jintao's data, it could be found that the abstract concepts in the target domains are commonly constructed and represented in terms of typically concrete concepts in the source domains as well, and some of the source domains have been found to be particularly dominant and widespread, which include the domain of JOURNEY, HUMAN, WAR, FAMILY, BUILDING and CIRCLE. In what follows, the source domains in Chinese data are to be described and analyzed in great detail.

4.2.1 JOURNEY metaphor

The essence of the socialism with Chinese characteristics is reform and development, building our country into a prosperous, democratic, highly civilized and harmonious modern socialist country. Like other developing countries, China has many challenges of unbalanced development in industrial structure between coast and inland regions, and between urban and rural areas.

However, since the purpose of JOURNEY metaphors is to raise morale and create a feeling of optimism, they are also frequently goal-focused and refer explicitly to the end point, or destination, of the journey (Charteris-Black, 2011: 68). In general sense, the most fundamental values in a culture will be coherent with the metaphorical structure of the most fundamental concepts in the culture (Lakoff, 1980: 22). Thus, the conceptualization of the advancement of a socialist country as a person traveling towards a desirable destination should fall into the domain of the most basic shared knowledge that is deeply embedded in our culture.

It can therefore be concluded from the above evidence that in metaphorical term the entities in the domain of journey get projected onto the entities in the domain of social development in Chinese political discourse. The expressions such as "社会主义道路" (socialist road), "改革开放的历程" (in the course of reform and opening-up) and "全面建设小康社会征程" (the journey of building a well-off society in an all-round way) positively construct the achievements that Chinese government has made so far in terms of the entities that make movement forward possible. This is not an isolated case. In reality, Chinese language has many everyday expressions that are based on the categorization and conceptualization of a nation's development and rising as a long journey, and they are used not just for talking about development, but potentially for reasoning about it as well. The following sentences are some of the linguistic expressions of the metaphorical concept SOCIAL DEVELOPMENT IS A JOURNEY.

(51) 我们将坚定不移坚持中国特色社会主义**道路**。

We will unswervingly adhere to the **road** of socialism with Chinese characteristics.

(胡锦涛在国庆60周年大会上发表的重要讲话)

(52) 推动新形势下党的建设开创新局面，在全面建设小康社会**征程**上取得新成绩。

Push forward the construction of the Party into a new level in the new situation and make new achievements on the **journey** of building a well-off society in an all-round way.

(胡锦涛在全国政协新年茶话会上的讲话)

(53) 总结中国改革开放的**历程**，中国人民得出了一个不可动摇的结论，这就是中国过去30年的快速发展，靠的是改革开放。中国未来的发展，也必须靠改革开放。改革开放是决定当代中国命运的关键抉择，也是13亿中国人民的共同抉择。

A solid conclusion has been drawn from China's reform and opening up **process**, that is, the rapid development of China in the past 30 years is attributed to reform and opening up, and China's future development will also have to rely on reform and opening up. Reform and opening-up is a key decision that has shaped modern China. It is also a choice made by the entire 1.3 billion Chinese people.

(胡锦涛在早稻田大学的演讲)

(54) 澳门回归祖国以来的10年，是"一国两制"在澳门成功实践的10年，是澳门基本法顺利实施的10年，也是澳门各界人士积极探索符合澳门实际的**发展道路**、不断取得进步的10年。回顾澳门回归祖国10年来的不平凡**历程**，可以得出以下重要启示。

Macao has seen the successful practice of "one country, two systems" and a smooth implementation of the basic law since she returned to the motherland 10 years ago. Besides, during the period, people from all walks of life in Macao have been exploring actively the most suitable development **path** and with joint efforts, achieving constant success in that way. Looking back upon the extraordinary **journey** of Macao since her return to the motherland over the years, we can obtain the following inspirations.

(胡锦涛在澳门特别行政区第三届政府就职典礼上的讲话)

It is the normal case that a successful landing on an unknown destination generally calls for the use of a map or a guide, entailing that a traveler may be lost on the way if the map or the guide is absent. Similarly, but for the guidance of these socialist theories with Chinese characteristics at the present stage in China, such as 'Mao Zedong Thoughts', 'Deng Xiaoping Theory', 'Three Represents' and 'Scientific Outlook on Development', the road of China's construction could have been steeper and the 'traveler' would have spent longer time in reaching the predetermined destination. In addition, the metaphorically used words such as "方针" (guideline) and "精神" (spirit) in the following sentences all share the notion of 'map' or 'guide' which plays an important role on the journey and this therefore could be represented as the evidence for the conceptual metaphor SOCIALIST THEORY IS A GUIDE.

(55) 我们要全面贯彻党的十七大和十七届三中、四中全会精神，以邓小平理论和"三个代表"重要思想为**指导**，深入贯彻落实科学发展观……

We should fully implement the spirit of the Party's Seventeenth Congress and the third and fourth plenary session of the seventeen Central Committee, and take "Deng Xiaoping Theory" and the important thought of "Three Represents" as the **guide**, and thoroughly implement the Scientific Outlook on Development...

（胡锦涛在全国政协新年茶话会上的讲话）

(56) 全国各地区各部门和社会各界大力发扬"一方有难、八方支援"的**精神**。

All regions and departments of the country should promote the **spirit** that when trouble occurs at one spot help comes from all quarters.

（胡锦涛在四川召开的抗震救灾工作会议上的讲话）

(57) 我们将坚定不移坚持“和平统一、一国两制”的<u>**方针**</u>。

We will unswervingly adhere to the <u>**principles**</u> of “peaceful reunification” and “one country, two systems”.

(胡锦涛在国庆60周年大会上发表的重要讲话)

(58) 在这里，我郑重重申，中央政府将继续坚定不移贯彻“一国两制”、“港人治港”、“澳人治澳”、高度自治的<u>**方针**</u>。

Here, I reiterate that the central government will continue to unswervingly implement the <u>**guideline**</u> “one country, two systems”, “Hong Kong people governing Hong Kong” and “Macao people governing Macao” with a high degree of autonomy.

(胡锦涛在澳门特别行政区第三届政府就职典礼上的讲话)

Journeys are a potent source domain for metaphor because of the availability of a clear schema that includes required elements – such as start and end points connected by a path and entities that move along the path; this is usually represented in cognitive linguistics as a SOURCE-PATH-GOAL Schema (Charteris-Black, 2011: 66).

The SOURCE-PATH-GOAL schema has the following elements: a trajector that moves; a source location; an intended destination of the trajector; a route from the source to the goal; the actual trajectory of motion; the position of the trajector at a given time; the direction of the trajector at that time; the actual final location of the trajector, which may or may not be the intended destination (Lakoff & Johnson, 1999: 33). Within CMT, the use of verb of motion highlights movement and the use of ‘destination’ highlights goal-orientation (Charteris-Black, 2004: 74).

Similarly, in the course of a nation's construction and development, her people need to set out for a goal at first and then they get down to achieving certain purposes. Here the expressions such as "朝着" (the road towards) and "前进" (movement forward) positively construct what has been achieved in terms of movement forward. This also entails that the achievement that has been made is just part of longer process rather than the final desirable outcome; "宏伟目标" (a grand objective) highlights the worthiness of the motive for the journey. However, the journey isn't easy because there are impediments, and there are crossroads in which a decision has to be made about which direction to go for or whether to keep on travelling. The following examples are some of the evidence for the metaphorical concept BUILDING A WEALTHY AND HARMONIOUS SOCIETY IS TRAVELING ALONG A PATH TOWARDS A DESTINATION.

(59) 全国各族人民都为伟大祖国的发展进步感到无比自豪，都对实现全面建设小康社会的**宏伟目标**、进而实现中华民族伟大复兴充满必胜信心。

People of all ethnic groups in China are proud of the great progress in this great motherland, and they are full of confidence in realizing the **grand goal** of building a moderately prosperous society in an all-round way and thus achieving the great rejuvenation of the Chinese nation.

（胡锦涛在全国政协新年茶话会上的讲话）

(60) 继续**朝着**建设富强民主文明和谐的社会主义现代化国家、实现中华民族伟大复兴的宏伟**目标**奋勇**前进**。

We will continue to forge ahead **towards** the goal of building a prosperous, democratic, civilized and harmonious socialist modern country and realizing the great rejuvenation of the Chinese nation.

(胡锦涛在澳门特别行政区第三届政府就职典礼上的讲话)

It is the common knowledge that a journey involves investment of time and effort and movement of progress towards a desirable social goal is difficult because travelers may be involved in some form of short-term suffering or struggle on the way. In the case of Chinese political speeches, a wide range of social problems are commonly represented as the source of obstacles or burdens, including air pollution, population boom, unemployment, poverty, terrorism, natural disasters etc. However, our basic knowledge of what may prevent or hinder movement towards a desirable destination is always employed in Chinese political speeches to make a strong positive orientation for political ends:

It is then important to tolerate the burdens and hardships for the purpose of achieving long-term political goals because the terminal objectives are worthwhile. In this respect, the conceptual metaphor HARDSHIPS ARE BURDENS can be formulated through the identification of the metaphorically used words in the following examples.

(61) 同志们、朋友们！新的一年已经开始，艰巨繁重的**任务**正等待着我们去完成。

Comrades and friends! The new year has begun, and the arduous **task** is waiting for us to finish.

(胡锦涛在全国政协新年茶话会上的讲话)

(62) 14万6千名人民子弟兵，心系灾区人民安危，**肩负**党和人民期望，从高级将领到普通士兵，发扬英勇顽强、不怕牺牲、连续作战的战斗作风，**承担**起抗震救灾最紧急、最艰难、最危险的任务。

146 thousand people's Liberation Army, from senior generals to the ordinary soldiers, were concerned with the safety of the people in the disaster-affected areas. They **shoulder** the expectations of the Party and the people, carry forward the fighting style of bravery, tenacity, fear of no sacrifice and continuous fighting and **undertake** the most urgent, the most difficult and the most dangerous task in combating the earthquake and carrying out relief work.

（胡锦涛在四川召开的抗震救灾工作会议上的讲话）

4.2.2 HUMAN metaphor

It could be found that in Chinese political discourse we often make sense of an abstract domain of experience in terms of the domain of human characteristics as well. Specifically, a state is commonly being conceptualized as a person, engaging in social relations within a world community, with implications that the land-mass is her home, that it lives in a neighborhood, and has neighbors, friends and enemies. States are seen as having inherent dispositions: they can be peaceful or aggressive, responsible or irresponsible, industrious or lazy (Lakoff, 1991). In actuality one of the most basic of personification metaphors is an abstract property is a person whose salient characteristic is that property. Metaphorically, we understand the people as personifying the properties (Turner, 2000: 22).

In Chinese political language, for example, we may often treat a country as human being in expressions like "两国的友好关系" (the friendship of two countries), "经贸伙伴" (business partner) and "焕发生机活力" (present vigor and vitality). In addition, a nation can be conceptualized as a person who has gone through all the vicissitudes in his lifetime. Thus, the use of expressions such as "艰难曲折的道路" (a difficult and tortuous road), "历经沧桑" (go through all the vicissitudes of life) and "饱经磨难" (experience many trials and tribulations) can be found in Chinese political discourse. Consider the following examples,

(63) 澳门回归祖国10年来，在中央政府和祖国内地**大力支持**下，……使澳门这座历史悠久的商埠名城**焕发**出前所未有的**生机活力**。

Within the 10 years since Macao's reunification to the motherland, the central government and the mainland have vigorously supported it... make Macao the historic commercial port city with hitherto unknown vitality.

（胡锦涛在澳门特别行政区第三届政府就职典礼上的讲话）

(64) 同时，中国也**走过**了艰难曲折的发展道路。特别是1840年鸦片战争以后，由于封建统治的腐朽没落和帝国主义列强的侵略蹂躏，中国**饱经磨难**、**历经沧桑**。

China has also **traveled** a tortuous and difficult path in the course of development. In particular, after the Opium War in 1840, China **endured many trials and tribulations** because of the decadent and declining rule of feudalism and the ravaging aggression of imperialist powers.

（胡锦涛在早稻田大学的演讲）

(65) 中国坚定不移地**奉行**独立自主的和平外交政策，坚定不移地奉行互利共赢的开放战略，致力于推进国际关系民主化，推动经济全球化朝着均衡、普惠、共赢方向发展，促进人类文明交流互鉴，**呵护**人类赖以生存的地球家园，同世界各国一起**分享**发展机遇、共同**应对**风险挑战，推动建设持久和平、共同繁荣的和谐世界。

We firmly **pursue** an independent foreign policy of peace and a win-win strategy of opening up. We promote democracy in international relations, advance economic globalization in the direction of balanced development, shared benefits and win-win progress, facilitate exchanges among civilizations and **protect** the Earth, the place we call home. We share development opportunities with other countries and work with them to **meet** challenges and build a harmonious world of durable peace and common prosperity.

（胡锦涛在早稻田大学的演讲）

（66）到了近代，由于日本军国主义对中国发动侵略战争，两国**友好关系**受到严重破坏。

In modern times, **our friendly relations** were devastated by the war of aggression the Japanese militarists waged against China.

（胡锦涛在早稻田大学的演讲）

（67）中日互为最重要的经贸**伙伴**。

China and Japan have been the most important business **partner**.

（胡锦涛在早稻田大学的演讲）

（68）中日是一衣带水的**邻邦**，**两国关系**正站在新的历史起点上，面临进一步发展的新机遇。

China and Japan are **close neighbors** facing each other across a narrow strip of water. Our **bilateral relations**, which are now at a new historical starting point, have new opportunities to grow further.

（胡锦涛在早稻田大学的演讲）

(69) 双方应该**客观认识**和**正确对待**对方发展，相互视为合作双赢的**伙伴**，而不是零和竞争的**对手**；**相互支持**对方和平发展，视对方发展为机遇，而不是威胁；**相互尊重**对方的重大关切和核心利益，坚持通过**对话**协商**解决分歧**。

We should **appreciate and see** each other's development in an objective and sensible way and regard each other as **partners** of win-win cooperation, not **competitors** in a zero-sum game. We should **support** each other's peaceful development and see each other's development as an opportunity, not a threat. We should **respect** each other's major concerns and core interests and resolve differences through **dialogue** and **consultation**.

(胡锦涛在早稻田大学的演讲)

4.2.3 WAR metaphor

It is found that conceptual metaphors from the domain of war include the metaphorically used words such as "战胜" (defeat), "战略" (strategies), "斗争" (conflict) and "新胜利" (new success) in Chinese political context. WAR metaphors commonly have an important role in the evaluation of abstract social goals. They are frequently employed by our leaders because they highlight the personal sacrifice and physical struggle that are necessary to achieve social goals, with implication that some form of short-term hardship is necessary to attain the worthwhile long-term goal (Charteris-Black, 2004: 69).

For this reason, we argue that WAR metaphors in Chinese presidential speeches always involve the mapping from the entities in the domain of war to the domain of a nation's development in which the government is being conceptualized as the commander, the people involved as the warriors, the way of making the country stronger is the strategy and the ultimate goal is to win the war. Therefore, the conceptual metaphor DEVELOPING A NATION IS A WAR could be constructed from the following linguistic expressions.

(70) 让我们进一步携起手来，高举中国特色社会主义伟大旗帜，顽强拼搏，开拓创新，团结前进，为全面实现"十一五"时期经济社会发展目标、**夺取**全面建设小康社会**新胜利**而继续奋斗！

Let us further join hands to high uphold the great banner of socialism with Chinese characteristics, work hard, forge ahead and unite forward for the full realization of the goal of economic and social development in the "11th Five-Year" period and for **a new victory** in building a well-off society in an all-round way.

（胡锦涛在全国政协新年茶话会上的讲话）

(71) 我国继续处在经济社会发展的重要**战略**机遇期和社会矛盾凸显期。

China continues to be in an important period of **strategic** opportunities for economic and social development and a period of prominent social contradictions.

（胡锦涛在全国政协新年茶话会上的讲话）

(72) 中国将始终不渝走和平发展道路。这是中国政府和人民做出的**战略抉择**。这个战略抉择，立足中国国情，顺应时代潮流，……

China is firmly committed to peaceful development. This is a **strategic choice** the Chinese Government and people have made in light of China's national conditions and the trend of the times...

（胡锦涛在早稻田大学的演讲）

(73) 历史启示我们，前进道路从来不是一帆风顺的，但掌握了自己命运、团结起来的人民必将**战胜**一切艰难险阻，不断创造历史伟业。

History suggests to us that the road of advance has never been smooth. But the people who control their own destiny and stay united will definitely **overcome** all difficulties and dangers and continuously create great undertakings in history.

（胡锦涛在国庆 60 周年大会上发表的重要讲话）

In addition, WAR metaphors are often used in relation to particularly serious and intractable problems, and to the initiatives and strategies that are developed in order to solve them. Conceptual metaphors such as these emphasize the gravity and urgency of the problems in question, and the seriousness of the effort that is being made to solve it (Semino, 2008: 100). This leads to the metaphorical expressions such as "抗震救灾" (earthquake resistance and disaster relief) and "第一线" (the battlefield).

From the perspective of CMA, the concept 'war' here is against such natural disasters as earthquake and floods that are negatively evaluated and therefore being conceptualized as 'enemy' in Chinese political context. Charteris-Black (2004: 92) suggests that there is a shared script for a ritualized sequence of activities in WAR metaphor: initially there is a threat – leading to identification of an enemy; then there is a call to action in which allies are summoned, a military struggle against an enemy.

CMA then shows evidence for the conceptual metaphors NATURAL DISASTERS ARE ENEMY and DEFEATING ENEMIES IS A WAR, with implications that natural disaster is a dangerous enemy that may cause huge economic losses, that the disaster-hit areas are the battlefield where our warriors are involved in a life-death struggle and that Chinese people should defeat them for survival. Consider the following examples,

(74) 人民解放军指战员、武警部队官兵、民兵预备役人员和公安民警以最快速度奔赴**抗震救灾第一线**，临危不惧，顽强**奋战**，争分夺秒解救被困群众，发挥了主力军和突击队的重大作用。

The people's Liberation Army, armed police officers and soldiers, militia reservists and police officers went to the **first line** of earthquake relief work at the fastest speed, facing danger fearlessly, **fighting** against troubles tenaciously and racing against time to rescue trapped people. All of them did play a major role as the main force and commandos.

(胡锦涛在四川召开的抗震救灾工作会议上的讲话)

(75) 只要全党**全军**全国各族人民众志成城、顽强拼搏，我们就一定能够克服各种困难，夺取这场**抗震救灾斗争**的全面**胜利**!

As long as the whole **army** and people of all nationalities unite like a fortress and work tenaciously, we will be able to overcome all difficulties and **win** a complete **victory** in the **fight** against the earthquake!

(胡锦涛在四川召开的抗震救灾工作会议上的讲话)

(76) 改革开放以来我国不断增强的综合国力，是我们**战胜**四川汶川特大地震灾害的坚实物质基础。

Since the reform and opening to the outside world, China's growing overall national strength has been a solid material foundation for us to **overcome** the devastating Wenchuan earthquake in

Sichuan.

(胡锦涛在四川召开的抗震救灾工作会议上的讲话)

"指挥部"(headquarter)、"突击队"(commando) and "保卫者"(defender) are commonly being employed in the description of war against the earthquake. In Chinese political language, it is important to see that we don't just talk about protection in terms of the entities in war, but, potentially, think and even reason about it in the same manner. Therefore, we are suggesting that many of the things we do in protection are partially structured by the concept of war. Technically, the partial slots in the category of conflict between human beings and nature get mapped onto the slots in the category of protection.

In fact, the analysis of WAR metaphor can be divided into three subcategories: metaphors of defense, metaphors of attack and metaphors of struggle. This classification can be done on the basis of the semantic orientation of the metaphor keyword. For example, 'fight' is an 'attack' metaphor when it collocates with 'against' and a 'defence' metaphor when it collocates with 'for' (Charteris-Black, 2004: 69).

Moreover, in WAR metaphor, we can see that the government and the Central Committee of Communist Party are often being conceptualized as commanders whose responsibility is to observe the situation, making critical decisions and strategies, giving orders and encouraging the army and the citizens to be perseverant till victory; the soldiers in the army are fighting against the enemy under their command. Thus, we may formulate the conceptual metaphors GOVERNMENT IS COMMANDER and THE MAJOR FORCE IN THE WAR IS THE ARMY, which may partially structure the actions we perform in protection. Consider the following examples,

(77) 几天来，在党中央、国务院和中央军委坚强**领导**下，在国务院抗震救灾总**指挥部**直接**指挥**下，四川等受灾省份……抗震救灾正在有力有序有效进行。

In the past few days, under the **strong leadership** of the Central Committee of the CPC, the State Council and the Central Military Commission, under the **direct command** of the State Council's earthquake relief **headquarters**, Sichuan and other disaster-affected provinces... The earthquake relief work is being carried out in an effective and orderly way.

(胡锦涛在四川召开的抗震救灾工作会议上的讲话)

(78) 人民解放军指战员、武警部队官兵、民兵预备役人员和公安民警以最快速度奔赴抗震救灾第一线，临危不惧，顽强奋战，争分夺秒解救被困群众，发挥了**主力军**和**突击队**的重大作用。

The people's Liberation Army, armed police officers and soldiers, militia reservists and police officers went to the first line of earthquake relief work at the fastest speed, facing danger fearlessly, fighting against troubles tenaciously and racing against time to rescue trapped people. All of them did play a major role as the **main force** and **commandos**.

(胡锦涛在四川召开的抗震救灾工作会议上的讲话)

(79) 使人民军队始终成为人民共和国的忠实**保卫者**和建设者。

Make the people's army always a loyal **defender** and builder of the people's republic.

(胡锦涛在四川召开的抗震救灾工作会议上的讲话)

4.2.4 FAMILY metaphor

Since ancient times, Chinese people have always been living in a society of agriculture who treat family as the basic unit of life as well as a center for social activities. Chinese people emphasize family such that a wide range of social activities among them are family-oriented or family-driven as the philosophy of Confucianism has a profound impact on the establishment of a family-oriented society.

Given the dominant role of family life in Chinese culture, it comes as little surprise that a nation is commonly being conceptualized as a family in Chinese political language as well. It is because the Nation-as-Family metaphor is deeply taken root in Chinese people's mind and is basically consistent with the fundamental values and ideology in Chinese traditional culture, hence the frequent uses of expressions such as "家园" (homeland), "当家作主" (the master of a family) and "主人翁地位" (the master status) can be reflected in Chinese political discourse. Consider the following examples,

(80) 我们要进一步抓好灾后恢复重建工作，大力支持灾区人民重建**美好家园**。

We should do a better job of restoring and rebuilding post disaster, and vigorously support the people in the disaster-affected areas to rebuild their **beautiful homes**.

（胡锦涛在四川召开的抗震救灾工作会议上的讲话）

(81) 在千钧一发的生死关头，多少人瞬间作出把生的希望留给他人、把死的威胁留给自己的抉择，多少父母用双臂为孩子撑起生命的天空，多少老师用身躯为学生挡住死神的威胁，多少干部舍**小家为大家**、奋不顾身地奋战在第一线。

At the life-or-death moment so many people were determined to leave the hope of life to others in a flash while keep the death threats to their own; so many parents courageously held up the sky of life with arms for the children; so many teachers block death threats with the body for their students; so many cadres **sacrificed their small family for homes for everyone**, fighting in the first line regardless of the personal danger.

（胡锦涛在四川召开的抗震救灾工作会议上的讲话）

（82）从1911年到1949年，中国人民经过长期浴血奋斗，实现了民族独立和人民解放，建立了人民**当家作主**的新中国，为实现中国发展繁荣创造了根本条件。

From 1911 to 1949, after long bloody struggle Chinese people finally won their national independence and people's liberation and established a new China where **the people are masters of the country**, which lays a solid foundation for the development and prosperity of China.

（胡锦涛在早稻田大学的演讲）

（83）既要维护澳门特别行政区依法享有的高度自治权，充分保障澳门同胞当家作主的**主人翁地位**，又要尊重中央政府依法享有的权力，坚决反对任何外部势力干预澳门事务。

We must not only safeguard the high autonomy of the Macao Special Administrative Region in accordance with the law and fully guarantee the **master's position** of the Macao compatriots, but also respect the power vested with the central government and firmly opposed to any external force to interfere in the affairs of Macao.

（胡锦涛在澳门特别行政区第三届政府就职典礼上的讲话）

The frequent use of the metaphor NATION IS A FAMILY may arouse the image of the 'one-family' ideology in Chinese people's mind. It strengthens the ties of kinship that may burn people's love and strengthen the loyalty for their motherland and spur their strong will for the reunification of one nation. In FAMILY metaphor, the government, who acts as the parent, is to protect the family, raise the children and educate them to be independent and iron-willed adults. Thus, the underlying conceptual metaphor THE GOVERNMENT IS THE PARENT could be formulated through the following sentences.

(84) 在以毛泽东同志、邓小平同志、江泽民同志为核心的党的三代中央**领导**集体和党的十六大以来的党中央**领导**下，勤劳智慧的我国各族人民同心同德、艰苦奋斗，战胜各种艰难曲折和风险考验，取得了举世瞩目的伟大成就，谱写了自强不息的壮丽凯歌。

Under **the leadership** of the three generations of the central leading collective with Comrade Mao Zedong, Comrade Deng Xiaoping, and Comrade Jiang Zemin as the core, and the Party Central Committee since the 16th Party Congress, the diligent and wise Chinese people of all ethnic groups have worked hard with one heart and one mind, withstood the tests of all kinds of difficulties, twists and turns, and risks, made achievements, and written a brilliant and triumphant song of striving constantly to become stronger.

（胡锦涛在国庆60周年大会上发表的重要讲话）

The use of the concept “众志成城”（unity is strength) in the above examples suggest that the government is the parent in the family who always holds the most intimate relationship with her children and always stands with them to get through the hardships and difficulties that they encounter on the way to the predetermined destination; the use of “后盾”（backbone）indicates that a parent cares about the children and is responsible for their security, and is ready to support them when they are in trouble.

(85) 伟大的祖国始终是香港、澳门繁荣稳定的坚强**后盾**。

The great motherland has always been a **strong supporter** of prosperity and stability in Hongkong and Macao.

(胡锦涛在澳门特别行政区第三届政府就职典礼上的讲话)

(86) 在同特大地震灾害的艰苦搏斗中，我们的党、我们的军队、我们的人民万众一心、**众志成城**，充分展现了中华民族和衷共济、团结奋斗的民族品格。

In a hard struggle with the earthquake disaster, our Party, our army and our people **unite like a fortress**, which fully demonstrate the national character: work together with one heart.

(胡锦涛在四川召开的抗震救灾工作会议上的讲话)

Since government is commonly being conceptualized as parent and her citizens naturally correspond to the sons and daughters in the family. The uses of the expressions such as "儿女" (sons and daughters) and "同胞" (brothers and sisters) may strengthen the sense of belonging to their motherland and burn the patriotism to contribute to the construction of their nation.

(87) 团结前进，就是要加强全党的团结、全国各族人民的团结、海内外中华**儿女**的团结，形成共克时艰、共创伟业的强大力量，为祖国发展进步、为中华民族伟大复兴不懈奋斗！

By "unity and forward" we mean strengthening the unity of the Party, of the people of all nationalities and of **the sons and** daughters both at home and abroad, which shapes the powerful force to overcome difficulties and create great cause together for the progress and development of the motherland and for the great rejuvenation of the Chinese nation!

(胡锦涛在澳门特别行政区第三届政府就职典礼上的讲话)

(88) 澳门回归祖国，实现了包括广大澳门**同胞**在内的全国各族人民的夙愿，标志着澳门**同胞**从此真正成为这块土地上的主人，澳门从此进入历史发展新纪元。

Macao's reunification with the motherland makes the long-cherished wish of the people of all ethnic groups including Macao **compatriots** come true, which marks that the Macao compatriots have truly become the land owner and that Macao has entered a new era in the history of development.

(胡锦涛在澳门特别行政区第三届政府就职典礼上的讲话)

When brothers and sisters stand together, they are invincible. Compatriots on both sides of the Straits must work together if we are to achieve the great rejuvenation of the Chinese nation. Promoting the peaceful development of cross-Straits relations hand in hand and achieving the great rejuvenation of the Chinese nation with one heart should become the theme of cross-Straits relations and the common mission of the Chinese people on both sides of the Straits. Our compatriots in the special administrative regions of Hong Kong and Macao need to put the overall interests of the country and their regions first and work together with all Chinese to safeguard and promote lasting prosperity and stability in Hong Kong and Macao. Our compatriots in Taiwan and on the China's mainland need to join hands in supporting, maintaining, and promoting the peaceful development of cross-Straits relations, improving people's lives on both sides, and creating a new future for the Chinese nation (Xi, 2014: 64 – 5). Therefore, the metaphor COMPATRIOTS ARE SONS AND DAUGHTERS can be reflected in the above sentences.

4.2.5 BUILDING metaphor

Charteris-Black (2004: 95) argues that common ground could be obtained between BUILDING metaphor and JOURNEY metaphor, with the evidence that building and travelling are at first conceptually related and both of them belong to the category of activity where progress takes place in stages towards a predetermined goal and that both imply a positive evaluation of political policy with the precondition that achieving goals is inherently good.

He then clarifies the commonality between the two concepts from the perspective of topography: both involve increase in the surface that is covered; it is along a horizontal path in the case of JOURNEY metaphors and for BUILDING metaphors there is an increase along a vertical path. This explanation does not come out of thin air but of experiential basis of our human body, with reason that no metaphor can be comprehended or even adequately represented independently of its experiential basis (Lakoff, 1980: 19). Therefore, it can be argued that more of good things – achieving goals – are likely to carry a strong positive connotation.

We hold that human conceptualization and perception of the concept of building in Chinese data is basically consistent with what we know about the topic in English data as both nations are based on the shared experiential grounding. Therefore, we could naturally come to a conclusion that the lack of such basic infrastructure as framework and stuff of a building could possibly lead to the collapse of that building with disastrous consequences.

Moreover, it is obvious that there are some similarities between the construction of a building and a nation's development in Chinese data. It can therefore be maintained that in Chinese presidential speeches, the entities of a nation's development and rising are always being conceptualized as that of the construction of a building. This makes it possible that we could reason about a nation's development in terms of the construction of a building. Thus, the uses of the concepts "建设" (construct) and "重建" (rebuild) can be treated as potential metaphorically used words and two more metaphorical concepts, namely, THE DEVELOPMENT OF A NATION IS THE CONSTRUCTION OF A BUILDING and CHINESE PEOPLE AND SOLDIERS ARE BUILDERS are formulated in Chinese political context. Consider the following examples,

(89) 我们加强军队全面**建设**，加快中国特色军事变革，军队有效履行新世纪新阶段历史使命能力得到新的提高。我们对加强和改进新形势下党的**建设**作出全面部署，继续开展深入学习实践科学发展观活动，全面推进党的**建设**新的伟大工程。

We will strengthen the overall **construction** of the armed forces, speed up military changes with Chinese characteristics, and effectively improve the historical mission of the army in the new century and in the new stage. We will make overall arrangements for strengthening and improving Party construction in the new situation, and continue to carry out in-depth study and practice of Scientific Outlook on Development activities, and comprehensively push forward the new great project of Party **construction**.

（胡锦涛在全国政协新年茶话会上的讲话）

（90）我们科学开展评估和规划工作，及时制定有关条例、指导意见和规划，中央财政建立专项基金，组织实施对口支援，依法有序实施灾后恢复**重建**。目前，各项恢复**重建**工作全面推进，灾区人民正在勇敢地走向新生活。

We will carry out scientific evaluation and planning work, formulate relevant regulations, constructive guidance and plans in a timely manner, establish a special fund for the central government, organize and implement counterpart support, and implement the post disaster recovery and reconstruction in accordance with the law. At present, the rehabilitation and **reconstruction** work has been carried out in an all-round way, and the people in the disaster-affected areas are brave enough to move towards a new life.

（胡锦涛在四川召开的抗震救灾工作会议上的讲话）

（91）中国人民有信心、有能力**建设**好自己的国家，也有信心、有能力为世界作出自己应有的贡献。

Chinese people are confident and capable of **building** their own country, and are also confident and capable of making due contributions to the world.

（胡锦涛在国庆60周年大会上发表的重要讲话）

As we mentioned in President Obama's data, BUILDING metaphors carry a strong positive evaluation of an activity because its result is valuable and worthwhile. For example, the use of "构筑"（forge） emphasizes the Chinese collaborative effort which could be reflected in building construction where a large number of people engage in a single common purpose. As with JOURNEY metaphors, BUILDING metaphors capture the idea of a building as the symbol of a worthwhile social endeavor and highlight the need for patience since it also takes time and effort to construct a building, which again implies a need to make sacrifices and not expect instant benefits (Charteris-Black, 2004: 96). Consider the following example,

(92) 只要澳门同胞继续发扬光荣传统，在爱国爱澳旗帜下实现最广泛的团结，就一定能够**构筑**起澳门长期繁荣稳定的牢固**政治基础**。

As long as the compatriots in Macao continue to carry forward their glorious traditions and achieve the most extensive solidarity under the banner of patriotism and love for Macao, we will surely be able to **build** a firm political **foundation** for Macao's long-term prosperity and stability.

(胡锦涛在澳门特别行政区第三届政府就职典礼上的讲话)

Evidently the use of a wide range of BUILDING metaphors plays a crucial role in making positive evaluations of actions and purposes of government. BUILDING metaphors presuppose that a government creates the opportunities that her people become more creative and productive in the cause of socialism. In Chinese political discourse, the people and soldiers are commonly being conceptualized as builders of socialist modernization who contribute to promoting the economy and make efforts to achieve the goal of creating a harmonious society. Consider the following examples,

(93) 全面推进革命化、现代化、正规化建设，不断提高履行新世纪新阶段军队历史使命能力，我们就一定能够使人民军队始终成为人民共和国的忠实保卫者和**建设者**。

If we comprehensively promote the revolutionization, modernization and normalization, and constantly improve the capability of army historical mission in the new century and stage, we will be able to make the people's army has become a loyal defender and **builders** of the People's Republic of China.

（胡锦涛在全国政协新年茶话会上的讲话）

4.2.6 CIRCLE metaphor

In Chinese politics, the Communist Party plays a great important role in the independence and development of PRC, which always represents the development trend of China's advanced productive forces, the orientation of China's advanced culture and the fundamental interests of the overwhelming majority of the Chinese people. In Chinese people's cognition, the center is the heart that represents the most important part and is the position where the leader stands. Thus, in Chinese political language, the Party and Chinese government are in the central position and the center then refers to the Party and the government as well.

CIRCLE metaphors could be seen in such concepts as "核心"(core) and "中央"(center) that literally mean the center and the core in Chinese. The use of expressions like "党中央" (the central committee) and "领导核心" (the core of leadership) is intended to convey an image that the Communist Party is the ruling party in China that has been playing a crucial role in the course of socialist construction. Therefore, it could be found that "核心"(core) and "中央"(center) are commonly used to refer to the ruling party, and the underlying metaphorical concept THE COMMUNIST PARTY IS THE CENTER can be reflected in the following examples,

(94) 60年来，在以毛泽东同志、邓小平同志、江泽民同志为**核心**的党的三代中央领导集体和党的十六大以来的党中央领导下，勤劳智慧的我国各族人民同心同德、艰苦奋斗，战胜各种艰难曲折和风险考验，取得了举世瞩目的伟大成就，谱写了自强不息的壮丽凯歌。

Under the leadership of the three generations of the **central** leading collective with Comrade Mao Zedong, Comrade Deng Xiaoping, and Comrade Jiang Zemin as the core, and the Party Central Committee since the 16th Party Congress, the diligent and wise Chinese people of all ethnic groups have worked hard with one heart and one mind, withstood the tests of all kinds of difficulties, twists and turns, and risks, made great achievements, and written a brilliant and triumphant song of striving constantly to become stronger.

(胡锦涛在国庆60周年大会上发表的重要讲话)

(95) 在这里，我代表**中央政府**和全国各族人民，向全体澳门市民，致以诚挚的问候!

Here, on behalf of the **central government** and the people of all ethnic groups, I wish to extend my sincere greetings to all the people of Macao!

(胡锦涛在澳门特别行政区第三届政府就职典礼上的讲话)

(96) 在**党中央**、国务院和**中央军委**坚强领导下，全党全军全国各族人民众志成城、迎难而上，迅速展开气壮山河的抗震救灾工作，奋勇夺取抗震救灾斗争重大胜利，谱写了感天动地的英雄凯歌。

Under the strong leadership of the **Party Central Committee**, the State Council and the **Central Military Commission**, the Party, the army and the people of all ethnic groups unite like a fortress, rise above difficulties, launch a magnificent earthquake relief work quickly, courageously win great victories in relief and finally write a big brilliant and triumphant song of the hero.

（胡锦涛在四川召开的抗震救灾工作会议上的讲话）

The conceptual metaphor THE NATION IS A CIRCLE indicates that Chinese people live as a big family, that they are represented as spots around the center forming a circle and that other countries are spots that fall outside the circle. Therefore, it is a prerequisite that a nation opens a ‘door’ of the circle for the cross-cultural communication between China and the rest of the world. Thus, the use of the terms such as “打开国门” (open to the outside world) and “对外开放” (the opening up) tends to send a message to the word that Chinese people live in a harmonious ‘circle’, and they are willing to open their door’s and support communication within different cultural background.

（97）坚持**开放**，就是要**打开国门**来搞建设。

To persist in **opening up** means that we should **open our doors** to pursue development.

（胡锦涛在早稻田大学的演讲）

（98）我们将以邓小平理论和“三个代表”重要思想为指导，深入贯彻落实科学发展观，统筹城乡发展、区域发展、经济社会发展、人与自然和谐发展、国内发展和**对外开放**。

We will continue to follow the guidance of Deng Xiaoping

Theory and the important thought of "Three Represents", fully apply the Scientific Outlook on Development, and work to balance urban and rural development, development among regions, economic and social development, relations between man and nature, and domestic development and **opening to the outside world**.

（胡锦涛在早稻田大学的演讲）

We are suggesting that the use of the concept "凝聚到党组织周围" (gather around the Communist Party) includes at least three mappings in Chinese political discourse, namely, from the source domain of circle to the target domain of nation, from the source domain of Communist Party to the target domain of the center and from the source domain of citizens to the target domain of spots around the center. Hence, the conceptual metaphor CHINESE PEOPLE ARE SPOTS AROUND THE CENTER can be seen in the following examples.

(99) 要始终把增强基层党组织创造力、凝聚力、战斗力作为党的建设的基础工程，做到抓基层、打基础一刻不放松，把广大人民群众紧紧**凝聚**到党组织**周围**。

We should always treat the work of strengthening the creativity of grass-roots Party organizations, cohesion and combat effectiveness as a fundamental project of the construction of the Party, and even not relax for a moment on the work of grassroots unit and the foundation construction, and always **condense** the masses closely around the Party organizations.

（胡锦涛在四川召开的抗震救灾工作会议上的讲话）

(100) 大家要继续高举邓小平理论伟大旗帜，紧密**团结**在党中央**周围**。

We must continue to high uphold the great banner of Deng Xiaoping Theory and closely **unite** **around** the Central Committee of the Communist Party.

（胡锦涛在四川召开的抗震救灾工作会议上的讲话）

Chapter 5 Comparative Analysis and Discussions

This chapter focuses specifically on the comparative analysis of conceptual metaphors I have identified in the speeches by former US President Barack Obama and former Chinese President Hu Jintao such that we would be able to explore the similarities and differences between the conceptual metaphors in the two languages, distill the deep causes underlying different metaphor choices from the perspective of embodiment and prove that abstract thoughts and concepts in Chinese political discourse are fundamentally metaphorical in nature as well.

5.1 Comparative analysis

5.1.1 Categories of the conceptual metaphors in the data

In the previous chapter, I have identified six major categories of the most frequently used conceptual metaphors in English and Chinese data. Table 2 shows the number of cases in these categories.

Table 2 The statistics of conceptual metaphors in English and Chinese data

English data		Chinese data	
Category	Number of cases (%)	Category	Number of cases (%)
HUMAN metaphor	16.5%	HUMAN metaphor	16.6%
BUILDING metaphor	17.4%	BUILDING metaphor	13.2%
JOURNEY metaphor	18.2%	JOURNEY metaphor	29.7%
FAMILY metaphor	12.4%	FAMILY metaphor	10.8%
DRAMA metaphor	7.2%	WAR metaphor	10.3%
RELIGIOUS metaphor	28.3%	CIRCLE metaphor	19.4%

Table 2 provides the number of cases in each category of conceptual metaphors both in English and Chinese data and shows that: in English data, the dominant category is RELIGIOUS metaphor while in Chinese data the dominant one is JOURNEY metaphor; four common categories could be found both in English and Chinese data, in which HUMAN metaphor shares almost the same percentage. In addition, there are four different categories of conceptual metaphors that are unique for one data. CIRCLE metaphor and JOURNEY metaphor are frequently used in Chinese data, while RELIGIOUS metaphors are massively found in English data.

5.1.2 The same metaphors in the data

As we have mentioned above, the similarities between certain metaphorical concepts in English and Chinese political discourse do not come out of thin air, but originate from human experiential bases in the physical world. Americans and Chinese share a large part of physical and bodily experiences that give rise to abundant similar or even the same image schema or structures, it should come as no surprise that there exist the same metaphorical concepts both in English and Chinese data, such as, HUMAN metaphors and BUILDING metaphors. Table 3 is the manifestation of cross-domain mappings of the two same metaphors in different languages:

Table 3 The manifestation of cross-domain mappings of the two same metaphors

Source domain	Mapping	Target domain
Nation	⟶	Family
Other countries	⟶	Friends and partners
Constructing a building	⟶	Developing a country
Soldiers and builders	⟶	People

5.1.3 Differences between the similar metaphors in the data

Table 2 shows that there are four major categories of conceptual metaphors both in English and Chinese presidential speeches. However, some underlying differences of the similar categories could be detected from the perspective of embodiment and cultural factors through a careful examination of the metaphors. Liu (2002: 4) states that although the use of metaphor is universal, the choice of specific metaphors for making sense of the world is always culture-specific. In addition, Lakoff and Johnson (1980: 22) argue that our values are not independent but must form a coherent system with the metaphorical concepts we live by. In other words, we talk about things that way because we conceive of them in that way. Moreover, our conceptual system is grounded in, neutrally makes use of, and is crucially shaped by our perceptual and motor systems; we can only form concepts through the body. Therefore, the understanding that we can have of the world, ourselves, and others can only be framed in terms of concepts shaped by our bodies. (Lakoff & Johnson, 1999: 555).

The common knowledge is that speakers from different cultural communities find it difficult to understand or even reason about the way different people think as well as the related cultural implications, it would then be reasonable to argue that language arises from the interaction of both bodily and cultural experiences in the physical world. Thus, the dominant metaphors that speakers prefer to employ may provide a good channel for people from different cultural communities to conceive of the values and beliefs treasured in their own culture. Just as we have mentioned above, it could be seen that both of the two speakers use metaphors that are specific to their own culture to describe the abstract political concepts.

Table 2 shows that there are four shared categories of conceptual metaphors both in English and Chinese data, among which are JOURNEY metaphor, FAMILY metaphor, BUILDING metaphor and HUMAN metaphor. It is then assumed that both of the two leaders tend to choose the same image schema among different alternatives in constructing the abstract political concepts, but the difference could be reflected in the specific framing of different conceptual structures as well as the involvement of different participants. In English data, 'family' is basically constructed and realized in terms of different moral systems, namely, the STRICT FATHER model and the NURTURANT PARENT model. In JOURNEY metaphor, two presidents of both countries treat the development of the country as a journey, however, the differences could be seen in terms of the elements on the domain of journey that get mapped onto the domain of the development of a nation. In what follows, I will discuss each category of the conceptual metaphors in more detail to analyze these differences.

5.1.3.1 JOURNEY metaphor

JOURNEY metaphors are initiated by Lakoff and Turner (1989: 10) in the conceptualization of life, which at least include the following ontological correspondences in Table 4:

Table 4 The manifestation of JOURNEY metaphor

Source domain	Mapping	Target domain
A traveler	⟶	The person leading a life
Destinations	⟶	His purposes
Routes	⟶	The means of achieving purposes
Impediments	⟶	Difficulties in life
Guides	⟶	Counselors
The distance	⟶	Progress
Landmarks	⟶	Things you gauge your progress
Crossroad	⟶	Choices in life
Provisions	⟶	Material resources and talents

Table 5 Comparison between JOURNEY metaphor in English and Chinese data

Category	Conceptual metaphors in English data	Conceptual metaphors in Chinese data
JOURNEY metaphor	NATIONAL DEVELOPMENT IS A JOURNEY	SOCIAL DEVELOPMENT IS A JOURNEY
	FAITH IS GUIDE	SOCIALIST THEORIES ARE GUIDE
	COMMON PURPOSES ARE DESTINATIONS	ACHIEVING A HARMONIOUS AND WEALTHY SOCIETY IS THE DESTINATION
	DIFFICULTIES AND HARDSHIPS ARE BURDENS AND BARRIERS	DIFFICULTIES AND HARDSHIPS ARE BURDENS AND BARRIERS

By comparing the JOURNEY metaphors in English and Chinese data, we may conclude that JOURNEY metaphors are more frequently used in Chinese political speeches than those of America; the development of a nation is seen as a journey both in English and Chinese data, but the basic elements that get mapped are cultural-specific: in the Chinese political speeches the process of social construction and development is guided by socialist theories with Chinese characteristic such as "Deng Xiaoping Theory" and the important thoughts of "Three Represents", while in American political speeches, God's doctrine is the guide that leads American people towards a destination of prosperity and freedom. Table 6 and Table 7 present the similarities and differences between JOURNEY metaphors both in English and Chinese data through the ontological correspondence:

Table 6 The correspondence of JOURNEY metaphor in English data

Source domain	Mapping	Target domain
Journey	⟶	Development
Traveler	⟶	American people
Point of departure	⟶	The founding of the country
Luggage	⟶	Social problem
Guide	⟶	Faith
Burden and obstacle	⟶	Difficulty
Distance	⟶	Duration
Distance covered	⟶	Accomplishment of social construction
Destination	⟶	A nation of prosperity and freedom

Table 7 The correspondence of JOURNEY metaphor in Chinese data

Source domain	Mapping	Target domain
Journey	⟶	Development
Traveler	⟶	Chinese people
Point of departure	⟶	The founding of the country
Luggage	⟶	Social problem
Burden and obstacle	⟶	Difficulty
Distance	⟶	Duration
Distance covered	⟶	Accomplishment of social construction
Destination	⟶	Wealthy and harmonious society

JOURNEY metaphors that originate from human bodily experience as well as the corresponding cultural experience are frequently used by Chinese people for the conceptualization of such discrete and abstract concepts as "人生的归宿" (the destination of one's life), "人生的转折点" (the turning point of one's life) and "到达人生的目的地" (reach the destination in one's life). Moreover, these concepts are found to be abundant in classic literature in China among those well-educated men, for example, the expressions "读万卷书，行万里路" (To read great books and do great travels), "路漫漫其修远兮，吾将上下而求索" (The road ahead will be long and our climb will be steep) and "书山有路勤为径，学海无涯苦做舟" (Diligence is the path to the mountain of knowledge; hard-working is the boat to the endless sea of learning).

Lakoff and Johnson (1999: 178 – 9) maintain that our most fundamental understanding of events and causes comes from two fundamental metaphors which they describe as the Location and Object Event-Structure metaphors. What this mapping does is to allow us to conceptualize events and all aspects of them – actions, causes, changes, states, purposes, and so forth – in terms of our extensive experience with, and knowledge about, motion in space.

Thus, some of the reasons for the importance of JOURNEY metaphors in Chinese political communication can be attributed to the following factors: Journeys involve some type of physical movement from a starting point towards an end point; usually the starting point is in the present and is familiar or known while the destination is in the future and may well not be known. JOURNEY metaphors in political communication typically refer to the predetermined objectives of policy. They imply having a clear idea in mind of where one would like to be at some point in the future. Therefore, journeys imply some type of planned progress and assume a conscious agent who will follow a fixed path toward an imagined goal. Journeys are therefore inherently purposeful. It is this directionality that is important for political leaders who are conscious of the need to appear to have planned intentions. A leader who implied that policies would drift, would take the society nowhere or back to a place where it had already been would be rhetorically unsuccessful (Charteris-Black, 2011: 316 -7).

JOURNEY metaphor integrates basic cognitive schematic knowledge of daily experience of movement with other rich and varied knowledge of experiences that only sometimes occurs when we go on journeys. The expressive potency of the metaphors for leaders is because they integrate underlying positive experiences of successful arrival at destinations with the knowledge of what can go wrong. However, unlike say health and sickness metaphors, or life and death metaphors where the evaluation is fairly overt because we know health and life are good and that sickness and death are bad, JOURNEY metaphors are rhetorically successful because they rely on rich underlying cognitive patterns and on subliminal associations (ibid: 324).

Achieving the great rejuvenation of the Chinese nation has been the greatest dream of the Chinese people since modern times. It can be said that this dream is to make our country and our military strong. To achieve the great rejuvenation of the Chinese nation, we must both enrich the country and strengthen the military, and strive to build a strong national defense and powerful military. Finishing building a moderately prosperous society in all respects and building China into a modern socialist country that is prosperous, strong, democratic, culturally advanced and harmonious; and realizing the Chinese Dream of the great rejuvenation of the Chinese nation, in other words, making the country prosperous and strong, rejuvenating the nation, and making the people happy, deeply embody the ideas of Chinese people today and reflect our forefathers' glorious tradition of tirelessly striving for progress (Xi, 2014: 4 – 5).

In addition, I would like to emphasize a fact that the path of socialism with Chinese characteristics is the only way to achieve China's socialist modernization and create a better life for the people. This path both takes economic development as the central task and comprehensively advances economic, political, cultural, social, and ecological progress as well as other aspects of progress. The Chinese nation today is one which is undergoing great changes. Since the introduction of the reform and opening up policy, we have reviewed our historical experience and constantly made difficult explorations, and we have finally found the right path to achieve the great rejuvenation of the Chinese nation and our achievements have attracted the world's attention. This path is socialism with Chinese characteristic (ibid: 25).

However, building China into a modern socialist country is a long and difficult journey, where the Chinese government and her citizens need to work together to accomplish social constructions, solving social problems and overcoming any difficulty that they may encounter in order to achieve a prosperous, strong, democratic, culturally advanced and harmonious society. Thus, we are suggesting that it is not coincident that there are abundant JOURNEY metaphors in Chinese political languages, because they are deeply rooted in Chinese people's bodily and cultural experience, and they have become constant metaphorical structures of the most fundamental concepts in Chinese culture.

5.1.3.2 FAMILY metaphor

Table 8 Comparison of FAMILY metaphor in English and Chinese data

Category	Conceptual metaphors in English data	Conceptual metaphors in Chinese data
FAMILY metaphor	NATION IS A FAMILY	NATION IS A FAMILY
	GOVERNMENT IS STRICT OR NURTURANT PARENT	THE GOVERNMENT IS THE PARENT
		CITIZENS ARE SONS AND DAUGHTERS
		SOLDIERS ARE CITIZENS' BROTHERS

In the analysis of US politics, Lakoff (2002) extends NATION IS A FAMILY metaphor to integrate two quite different underlying approaches to morality that govern the conceptualization of social and moral problems in the United States of America. This metaphor portrays the government as parent and her citizens as children and thus allows us to reason about the nation on the basis of what we know about a family. According to his analysis, American politics is organized around two competing versions of FAMILY metaphor that are part of the conceptual systems of both liberals and conservatives. The moral role of the parents is to protect and provide for the family, and to prepare the children to thrive as independent adults. This role is represented in two very different ways, according to the parents' underlying view of reality, namely, the STRICT FATHER model and the NURTURANT PARENT model, which "induce" two corresponding "unconscious" patterns of moral belief systems, which, in turn, yield conservative and liberal world views. FAMILY metaphors are by no means a special feature of US political discourse. They belong to a common stock of political metaphors, which have been used in Western culture since antiquity (Musolff,

2004: 127).

According to Lakoff (2002), conservative political views are based on a STRICT FATHER morality. The strict father believes that life is difficult and the world is dangerous. The father must set strict rules to protect the family in a harsh world. In order for children to develop independence they must be rewarded when they do right and punished when they do wrong. Lakoff argues that conservative views on issues such as law and order, welfare, and education all derive from extending these views and applying them to the government's responsibility toward her citizens. While political liberalism is based on a NURTURANT FATHER model of the family that emphasizes cooperation more than competition and conflict. In this model, children are more likely to become responsible and self-reliant if they are cared for and respected, and if they are encouraged to care for and respect others. This view of morality emphasizes empathy, nurturance, compassion, self-nurturance, fairness, happiness and self-development (Ritchie, 2013: 179 - 180).

Surprisingly, Obama's administration adopts both the STRICT FATHER model and the NURTURANT PARENT model simultaneously in today's American political context, which shakes the very theoretical foundation of Lakoff's view on the moral system of the two Parties in American politics. We are then suggesting that, on the one hand, the government is represented as the STRICT FATHER of the big family who tends to impose disciplines or rules on children and teach them to tell right from wrong. The army is represented as the bodyguard of this family who obeys the order of the STRICT FATHER and protects the children. The government, on the other hand, acting as a NURTURANT PARENT, is more considerate and cooperative and cares about and acts responsibly toward their citizens.

However, family is regarded as a miniature of society and thus often attached great importance in traditional Chinese culture. Therefore, it comes as little surprise that FAMILY metaphor is a unique prominence in Chinese language (Liu, 2002: 55). For example, the use of expressions such as "兄弟姐妹" (brothers and sisters) may encourage her family members to emphasize and cherish the close relationship in the family and love each other as well; "祖国母亲" (motherland) may motivate people to love the country just as they love their parents; "大家庭" (big family), "当家作主" (the master of a family) and "家园" (homeland) may evoke the frame of people's responsibilities in their mind that they work and even sacrifice for their homeland. In addition, the government officials are often described as "父母官" (local magistrate) which literally means "father-mother officials" and, surprisingly, in Chinese, even the word "country" itself contains the concept of "family" as well, with the evidence that the concept "国家" (country) is an integration of two concepts, namely, "国" (state) and "家" (family).

Besides, as we mentioned in prior chapter, a nation is commonly compared to a big family with fifty-six nationalities living together where the president is often conceptualized as the parent of the family; "子弟兵" (the soldier) is represented as the son of the citizens which literally means "son-brother-soldier"; "军民鱼水情" (the army and the people are inseparable as fish and water) literally means that the army is the fish while the people are water; fish cannot survive without water. Thus, the figurative meaning of this expression is that our Party comes from the people, is rooted in the people and serves the people. Without popular support, none of the Party's achievements or aspirations would be possible. We must always keep close ties with the people, so that the Party can continue to respond to the challenges of governance, reform and opening up, and the market economy, as well as the external environment. Under no circumstances will we ever forsake our commitment to sharing weal and woe with the people. We will never forget the Party's purpose of serving the people wholeheartedly. We will never forgo the historical materialist viewpoint which regards the people as the true heroes. The Party will always serve the public, and govern for the benefit of the people (Xi, 2014: 403).

The mass line is the life our Party and the fundamental approach to the Party's work. Launching a program of mass line education and practice is a significant decision taken by the Party to supervise its own conduct and enforce strict discipline. It is an important measure to respond to public demand, to strengthen the Party as a Marxist Party that learns, innovates and serves the people, and to advance socialism with Chinese characteristic. It has far-reaching significance for the Party to maintain its progressive nature and integrity, consolidate its governing base and status, and complete the building of a moderately prosperous society in all respects (ibid: 401).

As has been the case throughout the Party's history, its close ties with the people are the embodiment of its nature and purpose, the hallmark that distinguishes the Communist Party of China from other political parties, and an important factor enabling the CPC to grow strong. The fate of the Party's undertakings relies on whether it can maintain its ties with the people (ibid: 403).

5.1.4 Comparison between the unique metaphors in the data

We have found that there are two major categories that are unique for one type of the data. In Chinese political discourse, the unique categories are related to WAR metaphor and CIRCLE metaphor, while in American political discourse the unique ones are DRAMA metaphor and RELIGIOUS metaphor.

5.1.4.1 DRAMA metaphor and WAR metaphor

Table 9 shows that in Chinese data the natural disaster 'earthquake' is considered as the enemy of the whole country that poses a threat to human life and maliciously destroys their properties. Therefore, the specific knowledge is that defeating the enemy is a big war, with the implications that Chinese people and officials are soldiers and that they need to fight against the enemy for survival and devote themselves to saving human lives and properties. In fact, Chinese people have long been educated and trained to be determined and brave when confronting natural disaster as they are fully convinced that natural disaster is ruthless and independent of human will but it can be defeated in due time.

So, only superior strength can defeat evil and only a show of strength can keep evil at bay. During the war time, the government is often represented as the commander, observing the intensity of the situation, making critical strategies, issuing every single important command and encouraging all her citizens to be confident and perseverant till victory.

In contrast, American people tend to take the sufferings as a drama of tragedy in which the government and her citizens are represented as actors and victims respectively, enduring irreversible physical pains and mental sufferings caused by the natural disaster. However, they have to "play" their roles well such that they could get through the hardships in the tragedy.

Table 9 DRAMA metaphor in English data and WAR metaphor in Chinese data

English data	Chinese data
DRAMA metaphor	WAR metaphor
	DEVELOPING A NATION IS A WAR
NATURAL DISASTER IS TRAGEDY	NATURAL DISASTER IS ENEMY
SOCIAL ACTIVITY IS A PLAY	DEFEATING ENEMY IS A WAR
THE GOVERNMENT IS AN ACTOR	THE FORCE IN WAR ARE THE ARMY AND PEOPLE
	THE WAY OF DEVELOPING A COUNTRY IS STRATEGY
	GOVERNMENT IS COMMANDER

5.1.4.2 CIRCLE metaphor

Lakoff and Johnson (1980) claim that, most metaphors, including structural metaphors and orientational metaphors, are grounded in systematic correlations within our daily experience. Through a careful examination of the entities and conceptual mapping process, I am suggesting that the unique CIRCLE metaphors in Chinese data basically originated from the typical Chinese culture and its political system: the whole nation is commonly framed as a circle with the government as the center; the citizens are around the government; the army is on the periphery to protect the citizens and the government. The center is the heart of the circle, and it ties the citizens tightly to form an unconquerable force that could go through any form of difficulties and defeat any kind of enemies.

China carries out a central administrative system, in which the central administration leads the local administration. The Communist Party of China (CPC) is the ruling party in China, and the other eight political parties are entitled to participate in the state affairs under the leadership of CPC. This political system reflects the conceptual system of Chinese people and links the use of CIRCLE metaphor in Chinese political speeches. In this connection, the cultural experience of China's political system allows us to understand, and even reason about the domain of "nation" in terms of the domain of "circle".

5.1.4.3 RELIGIOUS metaphor

Charteris-Black (2004: 173 – 4) argues that metaphor is the prime means of providing spiritual explanations since they can only be expressed by referring to what is experienced in the physical world. The topics that are dealt with by religion – the origin of life, suffering, the struggle between good and evil, life and death etc. – are also ones for which judgement and evaluation are often necessary. Metaphor in religion creates meaning by accessing subliminal experience because religion considers the possibilities of a sublime world beyond this world. Thus, it is hard to see how there could be a religion that does not involve the creation of a system of metaphors.

The rhetorical objective of choosing words from the domain of religion is to enhance the ethos[①] of the speaker because they imply that the political decisions are made on the basis of high principle rather than crude self-interest. Religious belief has always been an acceptable pretext for political action in American politics. This can be traced back historically to the early settlers and its presence in the wording of the American constitution (Charteris-Black, 2011: 217).

As Wander (1984: 158) argues that morality has regularly been

① Aristotle's views on rhetoric were based on the three artistic proofs of ethos (morally worthy), logos (proofs to support argument) and pathos (arouse feelings). Charteris-Black (2011: 14) constructed rhetoric means for persuasion in political communication, among which ethos was views as having the right intensions. That way that trust is established is by convincing the audience that the leader has the right intensions for the group and that he has their interests at heart.

employed in political rhetoric designed to appeal to the Protestant Establishment. The pragmatic effect of religious metaphors is to create a myth of political leadership as equivalent to spiritual guidance-in terms of the equivalence of principle on which both are presupposed. This entails a rejection of any clear-cut division of human motivation and behavior into the secular and the sacred (Charteris-Black, 2011: 218).

It should then come as no surprise that religion has a profound effect on political addresses in the United States in that America has always been a country of religion and most Americans are great believers in Christianity since the day when this country was founded. Just as we mentioned above, religion has played an important role in the development of the USA and Christianity has been an important source of interracial and inter-ethnic harmony. There is, then, no exaggeration to say that we could find its adherents and believers of different religions at any corner of this country. Therefore, religion may be frequently used as a source domain to regain and invoke spiritual aspirations into political context and to link the leaders with a promise to religious belief in this nation on the one hand, and meanwhile it may permeate every aspect of social life, customs, habit and even human daily functioning on the other.

In addition, Charteris-Black (2011: 218 -9) argues that RELIGIOUS metaphors fit well with other metaphor choices based on creation and rebirth; while for the purpose of analysis he has separated these metaphors into discrete categories, in practice they have a combined rhetorical effect on the audience. Choosing metaphors that send the same message, but from different directions, is an important skill of leadership because the effect is subtler and more difficult to detect and yet has a subliminal rhetorical impact on creating positive evaluations.

In contrast, the Communist Party respects and honors her citizens' freedom of religious beliefs in China. The religious policy, however, doesn't hold true for the members of Communist Party because they fall into the members of Marxist Political Party and they are atheist. Basically speaking, the Marxism is incompatible with any religious doctrines, and therefore, the members of Communist Party are not allowed to get involved in any form of religious activities. It then could be the reason for the absence of RELIGIOUS metaphor in Chinese presidential speeches.

5.2 Discussions

Through the comparative analysis of the conceptual metaphors in the political speeches by the two leaders, I am suggesting that conceptual metaphors are pervasive both in English and Chinese political languages. Political metaphors make it possible that abstract concepts in target domains get mapped from the domains of bodily and cultural experience, which allows us to understand and even reason about the abstract concepts without a systematic structure in terms of the concrete concepts which possess highly organized structures. Wang (2003, 2007) holds that there is not merely the use of the concrete to evoke the abstract, but also the employment of the concrete to metaphorize the concrete, the abstract to metaphorize the concrete and the abstract to metaphorize the abstract in Chinese. In contrast, the study shows that in Chinese political language there is only the use of such concrete concepts (the basic-level domains) as journey, human, building, family, war, circle to metaphorize and construct the abstract concepts. Therefore, it can be suggested that abstract political languages are metaphorical in nature because they are grounded in human bodily experiences of the physical world.

Chapter 6 Conclusion

With a comparative analysis of the conceptual metaphors identified in English and Chinese political speeches, I have listed the major categories of the conceptual metaphors in each data, explored the similarities and differences between these conceptual metaphors in the two languages, distilled the deep causes underlying the metaphorical concepts and proved that abstract concepts in Chinese political discourse are conceptualized and constructed in terms of cross-domain mappings and are fundamentally metaphorical in nature. This chapter presents the major findings, the implications and the limitations of this study in detail.

6.1 Major findings of this study

Overall, my discussion and analyses throughout this book have, I hope, demonstrated the following main points:

• Conceptual metaphors are pervasive in constructing abstract concepts in terms of concrete concepts in Chinese political language.

• In Chinese political language, there is no use of the concrete to metaphorize the concrete, the abstract to metaphorize the concrete and the abstract to metaphorize the abstract, but only the use of such concrete concepts (the basic-level domains) as journey, human, building, family, war, and circle to metaphorize the abstract concepts. Moreover, the abstract political language is metaphorical in nature because it is grounded in human bodily experiences of the physical world.

• The comparative study elaborates the embodied nature of the conceptual metaphors identified in the political speeches. It is found that there are generally eight metaphorical patterns in political speeches which are used to construe a large number of abstract concepts in politics, namely, human, building, journey, family, drama, religion, war, and circle. Besides, there are at least three relations among the conceptual metaphors in the political speeches in English and Chinese. Firstly, there exist the same conceptual metaphors in English and Chinese data: HUMAN metaphor and BUILDING metaphor; secondly, there are some conceptual metaphors that share the same source domains in the two data but with different realizations, namely JOURNEY metaphor and FAMILY metaphor; thirdly, there still exist some conceptual metaphors that are unique to one data, namely, the RELIGIOUS metaphor and DRAMA metaphor in English data, and the WAR metaphor and CIRCLE metaphor in Chinese data.

• The conceptual metaphors that exist both in English and Chinese data are dependent on human experiences of the physical world. With the cross-domain mappings between the bodily and cultural experienced domains and the abstract target domains, human beings have no difficulties or barriers in perceiving and understanding the abstract concepts without systematic structures in terms of the concrete concepts which possess highly organized structures. Fundamental to human thinking processes, metaphors act as powerful cognitive tools for our categorization and conceptualization of the physical world and play an important role in the construction of people's conceptual system.

- The similarities between conceptual metaphors in English and Chinese political languages do not come out of thin air; it is the natural outcome of the experiential bases of human social activities. Human conceptualization and perception of the world are deeply rooted in the shared bodily and cultural experiences, and therefore, there are abundant similar conceptual metaphors both in English and Chinese political languages.

- Human experiences are not isolated from the physical, social and cultural environment, and they tend to employ different source domains to understand and even reason about the abstract concepts in politics that the realizations of conceptual mappings are cultural-specific. Therefore, it comes as no surprise that there exist the differences between the metaphorical conceptual systems in politics within different cultural patterns.

6.2 Implications of this study

The book has a number of implications for diverse fields of study and application. On a general level, it has been a contribution to the further research on political language and culture both in English and Chinese and thus provides important reference values for cross-cultural communication, language teaching, and translation (e. g. corresponding transfer of conceptual metaphors in different languages and cultures). It also sheds some new light on the comparative study in other interdisciplinary field.

6.2.1 Metaphor and language teaching

Language comes out of a nation's long-term cognitive experience.

Foreign language learning involves two language structures, patterns and the representation of the experiential modes. Therefore, a systematic study of conceptual metaphors may assist students in mastering the basic analytical method of metaphor and developing their independent thinking and learning through the linguistic phenomena. In this connection, it is strongly recommended that priority should be given to the cultivation of students' critical thinking in language teaching and of the ability to learn how to conduct a comparative analysis of metaphors in different languages.

For example, through teaching the conceptual metaphor POLITICS IS FOOTBALL, students may learn how to analyze the evolvement of the relations between Italian culture and politics, which may further deepen students' perception of Italian politics and understand the nature as well as the history of Italian political system. Meanwhile, with an analysis of the prototypical case, students can be trained to develop the capability of exploring the nature of culture through complex language phenomena.

Moreover, metaphor is deeply rooted in human experience of the physical world, which plays an important part in constructing human conceptual system. The comparative study then can reveal the relationship between different languages and cultures such that students may have a better understanding of cross-cultural communication. Since people from different cultural communities tend to employ different ways of thinking to construe the abstract concepts, it is then a rational and effective way of integrating metaphorical thinking into the traditional foreign language teaching.

6.2.2 Metaphor and translation

The transfer of metaphors in different languages is hotly debated and much researched on the study of conceptual metaphor because translation is commonly viewed as cross-cultural communication that involves not only the transfer between languages, but also that between different cultural patterns. The emergence of CMT then provides a new method for the translation of metaphor.

Zhou (2003: 46) argues that the comparative analysis of two languages is pervasive in the process of bilingual transfer and that translation should be based on comparative analysis. He then argues that there is no good translation without a comparative analysis of the original texts and the target ones; without a comparative analysis of English and Chinese metaphor, the translation of metaphor is not possible. Liu (2008: 62) points out that concepts originate in the mind and it is not possible for people from different cultures to use the same figurative image to express the same concept. Therefore, the way that people express different entities differs; E-C translation of metaphor is not simply the stylistic correspondence of language, but a consistency of the two metaphorical concepts. Translation is not just a matter of language, but of thought. Metaphor is pervasive in political languages and through the comparative analysis of the data, people within different languages and cultural background will have a better understanding of the formation and the nature of political discourse as well as the underlying ideologies, based on which we could find a rational way of translating different political languages.

6.3 Limitations of this study and prospects for future research

In spite of the efforts made in this study, there is still some room for improvement.

Firstly, the collected data are based on five speeches both from former American President Barack Obama and former Chinese President Hu Jintao, which may not cover all the metaphorical expressions in political discourse. It is therefore not an exhaustive study of conceptual metaphors in the context of politics, and a larger corpus would be required in a quantitative analysis to test the claims made in CMT on the basis of inadequate linguistic evidence and verify the research findings in the book.

Secondly, the similarities and differences between conceptual metaphors in the data are tentatively explored such that the explanations may not be thoroughly convincing. Therefore, additional efforts should be devoted to distill the causes underlying similarities and differences between the conceptual metaphors in different data on the basis of the view of embodiment and culture.

However, corpora can provide an invaluable resource for the investigation of metaphorical patterns in language and for the extrapolation of conceptual metaphors from linguistic evidence. In fact, their increasing availability and accessibility make it less and less acceptable to use artificially constructed examples in order to make claims about metaphorical language use (Semino, 2008: 218). Therefore, the future study on metaphor should further improve the data collection and metaphor identification, making full use of computer technology to ensure that the concordances from the corpus would be able to thoroughly cover the word lists of the semantic domain (Liu & Cao, 2017).

Glossary

Conceptual domain. A conceptual domain is our conceptual representation, or knowledge, of any coherent segment of experience. We often call such representations "concepts", such as the concepts of building or motion. This knowledge involves both the knowledge of basic elements that constitute a domain and knowledge that is rich in detail. This detailed rich knowledge about a domain is often made use of in metaphorical entailments (Kövecses, 2010: 324).

Conceptual metaphor. When one conceptual domain (source domain) is understood in terms of another conceptual domain (target domain), we describe the cognitive phenomenon as conceptual metaphor or metaphorical concept. This understanding is achieved by seeing sets of systematic correspondences, or mappings, between the two domains. Conceptual metaphors can be expressed by means of the formula 'a is b' or 'a as b', such as ARGUMENT IS WAR, where 'a' and 'b' indicate different conceptual domains.

Conceptual system. Conceptual system refers to the repository of concepts available to a human being. The repository constitutes a structured and organized inventory which facilitates categorization and conceptualization. Each concept in the conceptual system can, in principle, be encoded and externalized via language. Concepts encoded in language take a modality-specific format known as a lexical concept. Cognitive linguists assume that language reflects the conceptual system and thus can be employed in order to investigate conceptual organization; they also assume that linguistic organization which is modified due to use can influence the nature and make-up of the conceptual system (Evans, 2007: 38).

Conceptualization. Conceptualization refers to the cognitive process of meaning construction to which language contributes. It does so by providing access to rich knowledge and by prompting for complex processes of conceptual integration. Conceptualization relates to the nature of dynamic thought to which language can contribute. From the perspective of cognitive linguistics, linguistic units such as words do not 'carry' meaning (s), but contribute to the process of meaning construction which takes place at the conceptual level (ibid: 38).

Correspondence. Within CMT, to understand a target domain in terms of a source domain means that we see certain conceptual correspondences between elements of the source domain and those of the target domain (Kövecses, 2010: 324).

Critical Metaphor Analysis. Critical Metaphor Analysis is an approach to metaphor analysis that aims to reveal the covert (and possibly unconscious) intentions of language users. The methodology typically proceeds by collecting examples of linguistic metaphors used to talk about the topic, generalizing from them to the conceptual metaphors they exemplify, and using the results to suggest understandings or thought patterns which construct or constrain people's beliefs and actions.

Embodiment. Embodiment involves people's subjective, felt experiences of their bodies in action that provide part of the fundamental grounding for language and thought (ibid: 325).

Hiding. In hiding, of the several aspects of a target domain, only some are focused on by the source domain. The ones that are not in focus are said to be hidden (ibid: 326).

Highlighting. In highlighting, of the several aspects of a target domain, some are focused on by the source domain. The source domain is said to highlight these aspects of the target (ibid: 326).

Ideology. Ideology is a system of beliefs and values based on a set of cognitive models, i. e. mental representations, including scripts, scenarios, frames, attitudes and opinions-partly linguistic, partly non-linguistic of recurrent phenomena and their interpretations in culture and society (Dirven et al, 2003: 1 –2).

Linguistic metaphor. Linguistic metaphor is the specific manifestation of its corresponding conceptual metaphor within CMT. A linguistic expression that, in context, is then used to refer to something that contrasts with (one of) its more basic meaning (s). This applies, for example, to the use of expression 'path' in the phrase 'long, rugged path towards prosperity and freedom'. Here the contextual meaning of 'path' (a specific method of gaining prosperity and freedom of a country) contrasts with the basic meaning (road). The contextual and basic meanings of a metaphorical expression belong to different conceptual domains, and the contextual meaning can be understood in terms of the basic meaning. In the case of the expression above, the process of finishing a difficult mission is understood in terms of a steep road.

Metaphorical entailments. Metaphorical entailments arise from the rich knowledge people have about elements of source domains. For example, in the ANGER IS A HOT FLUID IN A CONTAINER metaphor, we have rich knowledge about the behavior of hot fluids in a container. When such knowledge about the source domain is carried over to the target domain, we get metaphorical entailments (Kövecses, 2010: 325).

Mapping. Conceptual metaphors are characterized by sets of conceptual correspondences between elements of the source and target domains. For example, in the conceptual METAPHOR ARGUMENT IS WAR, the elements from argument corresponds to war. These correspondences are technically called mappings.

Ontological metaphor. Ontological conceptual metaphors enable speakers to make sense of their experiences in terms of physical objects, substances and containers. This understanding provides the basis for extraordinarily wide variety of ontological metaphors, that is, ways of viewing events, activities, emotions, ideas, etc., as entities and substances.

Orientational metaphor. Orientational conceptual metaphors allow speakers to organize a whole system of the target domain with respect to some human basic spatial orientations, such as up-down, in-out, front-back, on-off, deep-shallow, central-peripheral. Orientational metaphor gives a concept a spatial orientation; for example, HAPPY IS UP. The fact that the concept HAPPY is oriented UP leads to English expressions like "I'm feeling up today".

Personification. Personification is a type of conceptual metaphor that involve understanding nonhuman entities, or things, in terms of the characteristics and activities of human beings. They thus impute human characteristics to things. Personification can be regarded as a type of ontological metaphor (ibid: 328).

Scenario. Knowledge about a particular type of situation, including a setting, entities, participants, goals and actions, such as our knowledge of travelling on a train or being at a Party. Scenarios are a type of mental representation (Semino, 2008: 229).

Source domain. We use the source domain, a conceptual domain, to understand another conceptual domain (the target domain). Source domains are typically less abstract or less complex than target domains. For example, in the conceptual metaphor life is a journey, the conceptual domain of journey is typically viewed as being less abstract or less complex than that of life (Kövecses, 2010: 328).

Structural metaphor. Structural conceptual metaphors allow speakers to reason about the target domain in terms of the structure of the source domain. Such as ARGUMENT IS WAR, LIFE IS A JOURNEY. This cognitive process is based on a set of correspondences between elements of the two domains (ibid: 329).

Target domain. We try to understand the target domain, a conceptual domain, with the help of another conceptual domain (the source domain). Target domains are typically more abstract and subjective than source domains. For example, in the conceptual metaphor life is a journey, the conceptual domain of life is typically viewed as being more abstract (and more complex) than that of journey (ibid: 329).

Unidirectionality of conceptual metaphor. In conceptual metaphors, the understanding of abstract or complex domains is based on less-abstract or less-complex conceptual domains. With metaphors that serve the purpose of understanding, this is the natural direction; metaphorical understanding goes from the more concrete and less complex to the more abstract and more complex. The reverse direction can also sometimes occur, but then the metaphor has a special noneveryday function (ibid: 329).

English Bibliography

Aristotle. *Rhetoric and Poetics*, New York: Random House Modern Library, 1954.

Aristotle. *Poetics*, Michigan: University of Michigan Press, 1967.

Beer, F. A. & Landtsheer, C. D. (eds.). *Metaphorical World Politics*, Michigan: Michigan State University Press, 2004.

Black, M. *Models and Metaphors: Studies in Languages and Philosophy*, Ithaca: Cornell University Press, 1962.

Charteris-Black, J. *Corpus Approaches to Critical Metaphor Analysis*, New York: Palgrave Macmillan, 2004.

Charteris-Black, J. *Politicians and Rhetoric: The Persuasive Power of Metaphor*, New York: Palgrave Macmillan, 2011.

Charteris-Black, J. *Analyzing Political Speeches: Rhetoric, Discourse and Metaphor*, New York: Palgrave Macmillan, 2014.

Chilton, P. *Security Metaphors: Cold War Discourse from Containment to Common House*, New York: Peter Lang, 1996.

Chilton, P. *Analyzing Political Discourse: Theory and Practice*, London: Routledge, 2004.

Croft, W. "The role of domains in the interpretation of metaphors and metonymies", *Cognitive Linguistics*, 1993 (4).

Deason, G. & Gonzales, H. M. "Moral politics in the 2008 presidential convention acceptance speeches", *Basic and Applied Social Psychology*, 2012 (3).

Dirven, et al. *Cognitive Models in Language and Thought*. Hawthorne: Gruyter, 2003.

Evans, V. A Glossary of Cognitive Linguistics. Edinburgh: Edinburgh University Press, 2007.

Fauconnier, G. *Mappings in Language and Thought*. Cambridge: Cambridge University Press, 1997.

Fauconnier, G & Turner, M. *The Way We Think: Conceptual Blending and the Mind's Hidden Complexities*, New York: Basic Book, 2002.

Fitzgerald, S. *Spectators in the Field of Politics*, Basingstoke: Palgrave Macmillan, 2015.

Gibbs, R. *Embodiment and Cognition*, Cambridge: Cambridge University Press, 2006.

Gibbs, R. *The Cambridge Handbook of Metaphor and Thought*. New York: Cambridge University Press, 2008.

Glucksberg, S. & Keysar, B. "How metaphors work". In A. Ortony (ed.), *Metaphor and Thought*, New York: Cambridge University Press, 1993.

Goatly, A. *The Language of Metaphors*, London: Routledge, 1997.

Goatly, A. "Conflicting metaphors in the Hong Kong Special Administrative Region educational reform proposals", *Metaphor and Symbol*, 2002 (4).

Goatly, A. *Washing the Brain: Metaphor and Hidden Ideology*, Amsterdam: John Benjamins, 2007.

Graber, D. "Political communication: scope, progress, promise", In

A. Finifter (ed.), *The State of the Discipline*. Washington DC: The American Political Science Association, 1993.

Grady, J. E. *Foundations of Meaning: Primary Metaphors and Primary Scenes*, Unpublished PhD dissertation, University of California, Berkeley, 1997.

Howe, N. "Metaphor in contemporary American political discourse", *Metaphor and Symbolic Activity*, 1988 (2).

Johnson, M. *The Body in the Mind: The Bodily Basis of Meaning, Imagination, and Reason*, Chicago and London: The University of Chicago Press, 1987.

Johnson, M. *The Meaning of The Body: Aesthetics of Human Understanding*. Chicago and London: The University of Chicago Press, 2007.

Indurkhya, B. *Metaphor and Cognition: An Interactionist Approach*, Dordrecht: Kluwer Academic Publishers, 1992.

Koller, V. "'A shotgun wedding': co-occurrence of war and marriage metaphors in mergers and acquisitions discourse", *Metaphor and Symbol*, 2002 (3).

Koller, V. *Metaphor and Gender in Business Media Discourse: A Critical Cognitive Study*, Basingstoke: Palgrave Macmillan, 2004.

Kövecses, Z. *Metaphors of Anger, Pride, and Love: A Lexical Approach to the Structure of Concepts*, Amsterdam: John Benjamins, 1986.

Kövecses, Z. *Emotion Concepts*, New York: Springer-Verlag, 1990.

Kövecses, Z. *Metaphor and Emotion: Language, Culture, and Body in Human Feeling*, Cambridge: Cambridge University Press, 2000.

Kövecses, Z. *Metaphor in Culture: Universality and Variation*, Cambridge: Cambridge University Press, 2005.

Kövecses, Z. *Metaphor: A Practical Introduction*, Oxford: Oxford University Press, 2010.

Lakoff, G. & Johnson, M. "The metaphorical structure of human conceptual system", *Cognitive Science*, 1980 (4)(a).

Lakoff, G. & Johnson, M. *Metaphors We Live By*, Chicago and London: The University of Chicago Press, 1980 (b).

Lakoff, G. "Metaphor and war: the metaphor system used to justify war in the gulf", *Peace Research*, 1991 (23).

Lakoff, G. *Women, Fire and Dangerous Things: What Categories Reveal about the Mind.* Chicago and London: The university of Chicago Press, 1987.

Lakoff, G. & Turner, M. *More Than Cool Reason: A Field Guide to Poetic Metaphor*, Chicago and London: The University of Chicago Press, 1989.

Lakoff, G. "The contemporary theory of metaphor". In A. Ortony (ed.), *Metaphor and Thought.* Cambridge: Cambridge University Press, 1993.

Lakoff, G. & Johnson, M. *Philosophy in the Flesh: The Embodied Mind and its Challenges to Western Thought*, New York: Basic Books, 1999.

Lakoff, G. *Moral Politics: How Liberals and Conservatives Think*, Chicago and London: The University of Chicago Press, 2002.

Lakoff, G. "Metaphor and war, again", https://www.alternet.org/story/15414/metaphor_and_war, _again, 2003.

Lakoff, G. *Don't Think of an Elephant*, White River Junction, VT: Chelsea Green, 2004.

Lakoff, G. *Whose Freedom? The Battle over America's most Important Idea*, New York: Picador, 2006 (a).

Lakoff, G. *Thinking Points*, New York: Farrar, Straus and Giroux,

2006 (b).

Lakoff, G. *The Political Mind: A Cognitive Scientist's Guide to your Brain and its Politics*, New York: Penguin Books, 2008.

Lan, C. *A Cognitive Approach to Spatial Metaphors in English and Chinese*, Beijing: Foreign Language Teaching and Research Press, 2003.

Levinson, S. "Primer for the field investigation of spatial description and conception". *Pragmatics*, 1992 (1).

Littlemore, J. "The effect of cultural background on metaphor interpretation", *Metaphor and Symbol*, 2003 (4).

Littlemore, J & Low, G. *Figurative Thinking and Foreign Language Learning*, Basingstoke: Palgrave Macmillan, 2006.

Liu, D. *Metaphor, Culture, and World View: The Case of American and the Chinese*, Lanham: University Press of America, Inc, 2002.

Mac, C. *A Cognitive Theory of Metaphor*, Cambridge, Mass: MIT Press, 1990.

Miller, D. *The Reason of Metaphor: A Study in Politics*, London: Sage Publications Pvt. Ltd, 1992.

Mio, J. "Metaphor and politics", *Metaphor and Symbolic Activity*, 1997 (2).

Musolff A. *Metaphor and Political Discourse: Analogical Reasoning in Debates about Europe*, New York: Palgrave Macmillan, 2004.

Musolff, A. "Metaphor scenarios in public discourse", *Metaphor and Symbol*, 2006 (1).

Musolff A. *Analyzing Political Discourse: Discourse and Scenarios*, London: Bloomsbury, 2016.

Nimmo, D. R. & Coombs, J. E. *Mediated Political Realities*, New

York: Longman, 1987.

Pragglejaz Group. "MIP: A method for identifying metaphorically used words in discourse", *Metaphor and Symbol*, 2007 (1).

Reddy, M. "The conduit metaphor", In A. Ortony (ed.), *Metaphor and Thought*. Cambridge: Cambridge University Press, 1993.

Richards, I. A. *The Philosophy of Rhetoric*, Oxford: Oxford University Press, 1936.

Ritchie, L. D. "'argument is war': or is it a game of chess? Multiple meanings in the analysis of implicit metaphors", *Metaphor and Symbol*, 2003 (2).

Ritchie, L. D. *Metaphor: Key Topics in Semantics and Pragmatics*, Cambridge: Cambridge University Press, 2013.

Semino, E & Masci, M. "Politics is football: metaphor in the discourse of Silvio Berlusconi in Italy", *Discourse and Society*, 1996 (2).

Semino, E. *Metaphor in Discourse*, Cambridge: Cambridge University Press, 2008.

Sperber, D & Wilson, D. *Relevance: Communication and Cognition*, Oxford: Blackwell, 1986.

Taylor, J. R. *Linguistic Categorization: Prototypes in Linguistic Theory*, Oxford: Clarendon, 1989.

Thompson, S. "Politics without metaphor is like a fish without water", in J. S. Mio & A. N. Katz (eds.), *Metaphor: Implications and Applications*, New Jersey: Lawrence Erlbaum Associations Publishers, 1996.

Turner, M. "Aspect of the invariance hypothesis", *Cognitive linguistics*, 1990 (1).

Turner, M. "Language is a virus", *Poetics Today*, 1992 (13).

Turner, M. "An image-schematic constraint on metaphor", In R. A. Geiger & B. Rudzka-Ostyn (eds.), *Conceptualizations and Mental Processing in Language*, Berlin: Mouton de Gruyter, 1993.

Turner, M. *Death is the Mother of Beauty: Mind, Metaphor, Criticism*, Christchurch: Cybereditions, 2000.

Ungerer, F & Schmid, H. J. *An Introduction to Cognitive Linguistics*, Beijing: Foreign Language Teaching and Research Press, 2008.

Van Dijk, T. A. *Ideology: A Multidisciplinary Approach*, London: Sage, 1998.

Wander, P. "The rhetoric of American foreign policy", *Quarterly Journal of Speech*, 1984 (4).

Way, E. C. *Knowledge Representation and Metaphor*, Dordrecht: Kluwer Academic Publishers, 1991.

Xi, J. *The Chinese Dream of the Great Rejuvenation of the Chinese Nation*, Beijing: Foreign Language Press, 2014.

Young, H. *One of Us: A Biography of Margaret Thatcher*, London: Pan, 1993.

Yu, N. "Metaphorical expressions of anger and happiness in English and Chinese", *Metaphor and Symbolic Activity*, 1995 (10).

Yu, N. *The Contemporary Theory of Metaphor: A Perspective from Chinese*, Amsterdam: John Benjamins, 1998.

Yu, N. "Metaphor, body, and culture: the Chinese understanding of gallbladder and courage", *Metaphor and Symbol*, 2003 (1).

Chinese Bibliography

曹春春：《政治隐喻的文体功能探讨》，《福州大学学报》（哲学社会科学版）2008 年第 3 期。

陈勇、刘肇云：《隐喻政治与政治隐喻：论美国政治家的政治隐喻》，《外语教学》2009 年第 1 期。

贺梦依：《概念隐喻与政治的关系识解》，《外国语文》2011 年第 3 期。

贺梦依：《政治隐喻中的意识形态》，《当代外语研究》2014 年第 9 期。

黄敏：《隐喻与政治：〈人民日报〉元旦社论（1979—2004）隐喻框架之考察》，《修辞学习》2006 年第 1 期。

黄秋林、吴本虎：《政治隐喻的历时分析》，《语言教学与研究》2009 年第 5 期。

胡壮麟：《认知隐喻学》，北京大学出版社 2004 年版。

何自然、冉永平：《语用学概论》，湖南教育出版社 2002 年版。

蓝纯：《认知语言学与隐喻研究》，外语教学与研究出版社 2005 年版。

李玉萍：《俄语报刊政论文中隐喻的特点》，《解放军外国语学院学报》2000 年第 5 期。

李佐文、刘长青：《论隐喻的相似性基础》，《河北大学学报》2003

年第 3 期。
梁婧玉、汪少华：《政治语篇隐喻架构之分析——以布什和奥巴马的医保演说为例》，《陕西师范大学学报》2015 年第 2 期。
梁婧玉：《1946 年—2014 年美国两党政治语篇的隐喻架构分析》，博士学位论文，南京师范大学，2015 年。
林书武：《国外隐喻研究综述》，《外语教学与研究》1997 年第 1 期。
柳超健、曹灵美：《国外基于语料库的隐喻研究：方法、问题与展望》，《外语教学理论与实践》2017 年第 1 期。
刘法公：《隐喻汉英翻译原则研究》，国防工业出版社 2008 年版。
潘文国：《语言的定义》，《华东师范大学学报》2001 年第 1 期。
束定芳：《论隐喻的本质及语义特征》，《外国语》1998 年第 6 期。
束定芳：《隐喻学研究》，上海外语教育出版社 2000 年版。
束定芳、汤本庆：《隐喻研究中的若干问题与研究课题》，《外语研究》2002 年第 2 期。
束定芳：《论隐喻与明喻的结构及认知特点》，《外语教学与研究》2003 年第 2 期。
唐瑞梁：《概念隐喻映射制约机制》，《天津外国语学院学报》2007 年第 3 期。
吴丹苹、庞继贤：《政治语篇中隐喻的说服功能与话语策略——一项基于语料库的研究》，《外语与外语教学》2011 年第 4 期。
吴建伟：《政治隐喻对现实的除蔽与设障》，《华东理工大学学报》2012 年第 6 期。
吴建伟：《政治隐喻的说服机制与直觉过程》，《华东理工大学学报》2016 年第 6 期。
王晶芝：《元旦社论中的概念隐喻历时研究》，博士学位论文，东北师范大学，2012 年。
王晶芝、杨忠：《隐喻在政治新闻语篇中运用的可行性探讨》，《东北师大学报》2012 年第 3 期。

汪少华:《美国政府赖以生存的架构与隐喻》,《山东外语教学》2014 年第 4 期。

汪少华、张薇:《美国政治话语的隐喻架构模式建构研究——以布什和奥巴马的环保演讲为例》,《中国外语》2017 年第 2 期。

王文斌:《论隐喻中的始源之源》,《外语研究》2003 年第 4 期。

王文斌:《西方隐喻研究理论视点述要》,《宁波大学学报》2006 年第 2 期。

王文斌:《隐喻的认知构建与解读》,上海外语教育出版社 2007 年版。

王文斌:《论隐喻构建的主体自洽》,《外语教学》2007 年第 1 期。

王寅:《中西喻义理论的对比与翻译理论的建设》,《中国翻译》2000 年第 3 期。

王寅、李弘:《中西隐喻对比及隐喻工作机制分析》,《解放军外国语学院学报》2003 年第 2 期。

王寅:《语言能力、交际能力、隐喻能力"三合一"教学观》,《四川外语学院学报》2004 年第 6 期。

王寅:《隐喻认知理论的新发展——语言体验性论文之六:从神经学角度论证隐喻和语言的体验性》,《解放军外国语学院学报》2006 年第 5 期。

王寅、王天翼:《语言学新增长点思考之五:本土化的合璧式创新》,《中国外语》2008 年第 6 期。

王寅:《认知语言学》,上海外语教育出版社 2008 年版。

魏在江:《隐喻的主观性和主观化》,《解放军外国语学院学报》2007 年第 2 期。

文旭:《政治话语与政治隐喻》,《当代外语研究》2014 年第 9 期。

谢之君:《隐喻认知功能探索》,复旦大学出版社 2007 年版。

朱小安:《政治隐喻探讨》,《解放军外国语学院学报》2007 年第

2 期。

赵艳芳：《隐喻的认知基础》，《解放军外国语学院学报》1994 年第 2 期。

赵艳芳：《认知的发展与隐喻》，《外语与外语教学》1998 年第 10 期。

赵艳芳：《认知语言学概论》，上海外语教育出版社 2001 年版。

周志培：《汉英对比与翻译中的转换》，华东理工大学出版社 2003 年版。

Appendix I　Data Sources

English data

1. Barack Obama's Speech in Fudan University (November 16, 2009)

2. Barack Obama's Remarks on Recovery Efforts in Haiti (January 14, 2010)

3. Barack Obama's Remarks on National Independence (July 4, 2010)

4. Barack Obama's Remarks on Thanksgiving (November 26, 2009)

5. Barack Obama's Inaugural Address (January 20, 2009)

Chinese data

6. 胡锦涛在早稻田大学的演讲（2008 年 5 月 8 日）

Hu Jintao's Speech in Waseda University (May 8, 2008)

7. 胡锦涛在四川召开的抗震救灾工作会议上的讲话（2008 年 5 月 17 日）

Hu Jintao's Address on Earthquake Resistance and Disaster Relief in Sichuan Province (May 17, 2008)

8. 胡锦涛在国庆 60 周年大会上发表的重要讲话（2009 年 10

月 1 日）

Hu Jintao's Speech on the 60th Anniversary of the National Day (Oct 1, 2009)

9. 胡锦涛在全国政协新年茶话会上的讲话（2010 年 1 月 1 日）

Hu Jintao's Speech on the CPPCC New Year Tea Party (Jan 1, 2010)

10. 胡锦涛在澳门特别行政区第三届政府就职典礼上的讲话（2009 年 12 月 20 日）

Hu Jintao's Speech on the Inaugural Ceremony of the 3th Government in Macao Special Administrative Region (Dec 20, 2009)

Appendix II Sample Texts

English Sample Texts:

Barack Obama's Speech in Fudan University (**November 16, 2009**)

Good afternoon. It is a great honor for me to be here in Shanghai, and to have this opportunity to speak with all of you. I'd like to thank Fudan University's President Yang for his hospitality and his gracious welcome. I'd also like to thank our outstanding Ambassador, Jon Huntsman, who exemplifies the deep ties and respect between our nations. I don't know what he said, but I hope it was good.

What I'd like to do is to make some opening comments, and then what I'm really looking forward to doing is taking questions, not only from students who are in the audience, but also we've received questions online, which will be asked by some of the students who are here in the audience, as well as by Ambassador Huntsman. And I am very sorry that my Chinese is not as good as your English, but I am looking forward to this chance to have a dialogue.

This is my first time traveling to China, and I'm excited to see this majestic country. Here, in Shanghai, we see the growth that has caught the attention of the world – the soaring skyscrapers, the bustling streets and entrepreneurial activity. And just as I'm impressed by these signs of China's journey to the 21st century, I'm eager to see those ancient places that speak to us from China's distant past. Tomorrow and the next day I hope to have a chance when I'm in Beijing to see the majesty of the Forbidden City and the wonder of the Great Wall. Truly, this is a nation that encompasses both a rich history and a belief in the promise of the future.

The same can be said of the relationship between our two countries. Shanghai, of course, is a city that has great meaning in the history of the relationship between the United States and China. It was here, 37 years ago, that the Shanghai Communique opened the door to a new chapter of engagement between our governments and among our people. However, America's ties to this city – and to this country – stretch back further, to the earliest days of America's independence.

In 1784, our founding father, George Washington, commissioned the Empress of China, a ship that set sail for these shores so that it could pursue trade with the Qing Dynasty. Washington wanted to see the ship carry the flag around the globe, and to forge new ties with nations like China. This is a common American impulse – the desire to reach for new horizons, and to forge new partnerships that are mutually beneficial.

Over the two centuries that have followed, the currents of history have steered the relationship between our countries in many directions. And even in the midst of tumultuous winds, our people had opportunities to forge deep and even dramatic ties. For instance, Americans will never forget the hospitality shown to our pilots who were shot down over your soil during World War II, and cared for by Chinese civilians who risked all that they had by doing so. And Chinese veterans of that war still warmly greet those American veterans who return to the sites where they fought to help liberate China from occupation.

A different kind of connection was made nearly 40 years ago when the frost between our countries began to thaw through the simple game of table tennis. The very unlikely nature of this engagement contributed to its success – because for all our differences, both our common humanity and our shared curiosity were revealed. As one American player described his visit to China – people are just like us The country is very similar to America, but still very different.

Of course, this small opening was followed by the achievement of the Shanghai Communique, and the eventual establishment of formal relations between the United States and China in 1979. And in three decades, just look at how far we have come.

In 1979, trade between the United States and China stood at roughly $5 billion – today it tops over $400 billion each year. The commerce affects our people's lives in so many ways. America imports from China many of the computer parts we use, the clothes we wear; and we export to China machinery that helps power your industry. This trade could create even more jobs on both sides of the Pacific, while allowing our people to enjoy a better quality of life. And as demand becomes more balanced, it can lead to even broader prosperity.

In 1979, the political cooperation between the United States and China was rooted largely in our shared rivalry with the Soviet Union. Today, we have a positive, constructive and comprehensive relationship that opens the door to partnership on the key global issues of our time-economic recovery and the development of clean energy; stopping the spread of nuclear weapons and the scourge of climate change; the promotion of peace and security in Asia and around the globe. All of these issues will be on the agenda tomorrow when I meet with President Hu.

And in 1979, the connections among our people were limited. Today, we see the curiosity of those ping-pong players manifested in the ties that are being forged across many sectors. The second highest number of foreign students in the United States come from China, and we've seen a 50 percent increase in the study of Chinese among our own students. There are nearly 200 "friendship cities" drawing our communities together. American and Chinese scientists cooperate on new research and discovery. And of course, Yao Ming is just one signal of our shared love of basketball – I'm only sorry that I won't be able to see a Shanghai Sharks game while I'm visiting.

It is no coincidence that the relationship between our countries has accompanied a period of positive change. China has lifted hundreds of millions of people out of poverty – an accomplishment unparalleled in human history – while playing a larger role in global events. And the United States has seen our economy grow along with the standard of living enjoyed by our people, while bringing the Cold War to a successful conclusion.

There is a Chinese proverb: "Consider the past, and you shall know the future". Surely, we have known setbacks and challenges over the last 30 years. Our relationship has not been without disagreement and difficulty. But the notion that we must be adversaries is not predestined – not when we consider the past. Indeed, because of our cooperation, both the United States and China are more prosperous and more secure. We have seen what is possible when we build upon our mutual interests, and engage on the basis of mutual respect.

And yet the success of that engagement depends upon understanding – on sustaining an open dialogue, and learning about one another and from one another. For just as that American table tennis player pointed out – we share much in common as human beings, but our countries are different in certain ways.

I believe that each country must chart its own course. China is an ancient nation, with a deeply rooted culture. The United States, by comparison, is a young nation, whose culture is determined by the many different immigrants who have come to our shores, and by the founding documents that guide our democracy.

Those documents put forward a simple vision of human affairs, and they enshrine several core principles – that all men and women are created equal, and possess certain fundamental rights; that government should reflect the will of the people and respond to their wishes; that commerce should be open, information freely accessible; and that laws, and not simply men, should guarantee the administration of justice.

Of course, the story of our nation is not without its difficult chapters. In many ways – over many years – we have struggled to advance the promise of these principles to all of our people, and to forge a more perfect union. We fought a very painful civil war, and freed a portion of our population from slavery. It took time for women to be extended the right to vote, workers to win the right to organize, and for immigrants from different corners of the globe to be fully embraced. Even after they were freed, African Americans persevered through conditions that were separate and not equal, before winning full and equal rights.

None of this was easy. But we made progress because of our belief in those core principles, which have served as our compass through the darkest of storms. That is why Lincoln could stand up in the midst of civil war and declare it a struggle to see whether any nation, conceived in liberty, and "dedicated to the proposition that all men are created equal" could long endure. That is why Dr. Martin Luther King could stand on the steps of the Lincoln Memorial and ask that our nation live out the true meaning of its creed. That's why immigrants from China to Kenya could find a home on our shores; why opportunity is available to all who would work for it; and why someone like me, who less than 50 years ago would have had trouble voting in some parts of America, is now able to serve as its President.

And that is why America will always speak out for these core principles around the world. We do not seek to impose any system of government on any other nation, but we also don't believe that the principles that we stand for are unique to our nation. These freedoms of expression and worship – of access to information and political participation-we believe are universal rights. They should be available to all people, including ethnic and religious minorities – whether they are in the United States, China, or any nation. Indeed, it is that respect for universal rights that guides America's openness to other countries; our respect for different cultures; our commitment to international law; and our faith in the future.

These are all things that you should know about America. I also know that we have much to learn about China. Looking around at this magnificent city – and looking around this room – I do believe that our nations hold something important in common, and that is a belief in the future. Neither the United States nor China is content to rest on our achievements. For while China is an ancient nation, you are also clearly looking ahead with confidence, ambition, and a commitment to see that tomorrow's generation can do better than today's.

In addition to your growing economy, we admire China's extraordinary commitment to science and research – a commitment borne out in everything from the infrastructure you build to the technology you use. China is now the world's largest Internet user – which is why we were so pleased to include the Internet as a part of today's event. This country now has the world's largest mobile phone network, and it is investing in the new forms of energy that can both sustain growth and combat climate change and I'm looking forward to deepening the partnership between the United States and China in this critical area tomorrow. But above all, I see China's future in you – young people whose talent and dedication and dreams will do so much to help shape the 21st century.

I've said many times that I believe that our world is now fundamentally interconnected. The jobs we do, the prosperity we build, the environment we protect, the security that we seek – all of these things are shared. And given that interconnection, power in the 21st century is no longer a zero-sum game; one country's success need not come at the expense of another. And that is why the United States insists we do not seek to contain China's rise. On the contrary, we welcome China as a strong and prosperous and successful member of the community of nations – a China that draws on the rights, strengths, and creativity of individual Chinese like you.

To return to the proverb – consider the past. We know that more is to be gained when great powers cooperate than when they collide. That is a lesson that human beings have learned time and again, and that is the example of the history between our nations. And I believe strongly that cooperation must go beyond our government. It must be rooted in our people – in the studies we share, the business that we do, the knowledge that we gain, and even in the sports that we play. And these bridges must be built by young men and women just like you and your counterparts in America.

That's why I'm pleased to announce that the United States will dramatically expand the number of our students who study in China to 100,000. And these exchanges mark a clear commitment to build ties among our people, as surely as you will help determine the destiny of the 21st century. And I'm absolutely confident that America has no better ambassadors to offer than our young people. For they, just like you, are filled with talent and energy and optimism about the history that is yet to be written.

So let this be the next step in the steady pursuit of cooperation that will serve our nations, and the world. And if there's one thing that we can take from today's dialogue, I hope that it is a commitment to continue this dialogue going forward.

So thank you very much.

Barack Obama's inaugural address

My fellow citizens: I stand here today humbled by the task before us, grateful for the trust you've bestowed, mindful of the sacrifices borne by our ancestors.

I thank President Bush for his service to our nation as well as the generosity and cooperation he has shown throughout this transition.

Forty-four Americans have now taken the presidential oath. The words have been spoken during rising tides of prosperity and the still waters of peace. Yet, every so often, the oath is taken amidst gathering clouds and raging storms. At these moments, America has carried on not simply because of the skill or vision of those in high office, but because we, the people, have remained faithful to the ideals of our forebears and true to our founding documents.

So it has been; so it must be with this generation of Americans.

That we are in the midst of crisis is now well understood. Our nation is at war against a far-reaching network of violence and hatred. Our economy is badly weakened, a consequence of greed and irresponsibility on the part of some, but also our collective failure to make hard choices and prepare the nation for a new age. Homes have been lost, jobs shed, businesses shuttered. Our health care is too costly, our schools fail too many – and each day brings further evidence that the ways we use energy strengthen our adversaries and threaten our planet.

These are the indicators of crisis, subject to data and statistics. Less measurable, but no less profound, is a sapping of confidence across our land; a nagging fear that America's decline is inevitable, that the next generation must lower its sights.

Today I say to you that the challenges we face are real. They are serious and they are many. They will not be met easily or in a short span of time. But know this America: They will be met.

On this day, we gather because we have chosen hope over fear, unity of purpose over conflict and discord. On this day, we come to proclaim an end to the petty grievances and false promises, the recriminations and worn-out dogmas that for far too long have strangled our politics. We remain a young nation. But in the words of Scripture, the time has come to set aside childish things. The time has come to reaffirm our enduring spirit; to choose our better history; to carry forward that precious gift, that noble idea passed on from generation to generation: the God-given promise that all are equal, all are free, and all deserve a chance to pursue their full measure of happiness.

In reaffirming the greatness of our nation we understand that greatness is never a given. It must be earned. Our journey has never been one of short-cuts or settling for less. It has not been the path for the faint-hearted, for those that prefer leisure over work, or seek only the pleasures of riches and fame. Rather, it has been the risk-takers, the doers, the makers of things – some celebrated, but more often men and women obscure in their labor – who have carried us up the long, rugged path towards prosperity and freedom.

For us, they packed up their few worldly possessions and traveled across oceans in search of a new life. For us, they toiled in sweatshops, and settled the West, endured the lash of the whip, and plowed the hard earth. For us, they fought and died in places like Concord and Gettysburg, Normandy and Khe Sahn.

Time and again these men and women struggled and sacrificed and worked till their hands were raw so that we might live a better life. They saw America as bigger than the sum of our individual ambitions, greater than all the differences of birth or wealth or faction.

This is the journey we continue today. We remain the most prosperous, powerful nation on Earth. Our workers are no less productive than when this crisis began. Our minds are no less inventive, our goods and services no less needed than they were last week, or last month, or last year. Our capacity remains undiminished. But our time of standing pat, of protecting narrow interests and putting off unpleasant decisions-that time has surely passed. Starting today, we must pick ourselves up, dust ourselves off, and begin again the work of remaking America.

For everywhere we look, there is work to be done. The state of our economy calls for action, bold and swift. And we will act, not only to create new jobs, but to lay a new foundation for growth. We will build the roads and bridges, the electric grids and digital lines that feed our commerce and bind us together. We' ll restore science to its rightful place, and wield technology's wonders to raise health care's quality and lower its cost. We will harness the sun and the winds and the soil to fuel our cars and run our factories. And we will transform our schools and colleges and universities to meet the demands of a new age. All this we can do. All this we will do.

Now, there are some who question the scale of our ambitions, who suggest that our system cannot tolerate too many big plans. Their memories are short, for they have forgotten what this country has already done, what free men and women can achieve when imagination is joined to common purpose, and necessity to courage. What the cynics fail to understand is that the ground has shifted beneath them, that the stale political arguments that have consumed us for so long no longer apply.

The question we ask today is not whether our government is too big or too small, but whether it works – whether it helps families find jobs at a decent wage, care they can afford, a retirement that is dignified. Where the answer is yes, we intend to move forward. Where the answer is no, programs will end. And those of us who manage the public's dollars will be held to account, to spend wisely, reform bad habits, and do our business in the light of day, because only then can we restore the vital trust between a people and their government.

Nor is the question before us whether the market is a force for good or ill. Its power to generate wealth and expand freedom is unmatched. But this crisis has reminded us that without a watchful eye, the market can spin out of control. The nation cannot prosper long when it favors only the prosperous. The success of our economy has always depended not just on the size of our gross domestic product, but on the reach of our prosperity, on the ability to extend opportunity to every willing heart – not out of charity, but because it is the surest route to our common good.

As for our common defense, we reject as false the choice between our safety and our ideals. Our founding fathers, faced with perils that we can scarcely imagine, drafted a charter to assure the rule of law and the rights of man – a charter expanded by the blood of generations. Those ideals still light the world, and we will not give them up for expedience sake.

And so, to all the other peoples and governments who are watching today, from the grandest capitals to the small village where my father was born, know that America is a friend of each nation, and every man, woman and child who seeks a future of peace and dignity. And we are ready to lead once more.

Recall that earlier generations faced down fascism and communism not just with missiles and tanks, but with the sturdy alliances and enduring convictions. They understood that our power alone cannot protect us, nor does it entitle us to do as we please. Instead they knew that our power grows through its prudent use; our security emanates from the justness of our cause, the force of our example, the tempering qualities of humility and restraint.

We are the keepers of this legacy. Guided by these principles once more we can meet those new threats that demand even greater effort, even greater cooperation and understanding between nations. We will begin to responsibly leave Iraq to its people and forge a hard-earned peace in Afghanistan. With old friends and former foes, we'll work tirelessly to lessen the nuclear threat, and roll back the specter of a warming planet.

We will not apologize for our way of life, nor will we waver in its defense. And for those who seek to advance their aims by inducing terror and slaughtering innocents, we say to you now that our spirit is stronger and cannot be broken – you cannot outlast us, and we will defeat you.

For we know that our patchwork heritage is a strength, not a weakness. We are a nation of Christians and Muslims, Jews and Hindus, and non-believers. We are shaped by every language and culture, drawn from every end of this Earth; and because we have tasted the bitter swill of civil war and segregation, and emerged from that dark chapter stronger and more united, we cannot help but believe that the old hatreds shall someday pass; that the lines of tribe shall soon dissolve; that as the world grows smaller, our common humanity shall reveal itself; and that America must play its role in ushering in a new era of peace.

To the Muslim world, we seek a new way forward, based on mutual interest and mutual respect. To those leaders around the globe who seek to sow conflict, or blame their society's ills on the West, know that your people will judge you on what you can build, not what you destroy.

To those who cling to power through corruption and deceit and the silencing of dissent, know that you are on the wrong side of history, but that we will extend a hand if you are willing to unclench your fist.

To the people of poor nations, we pledge to work alongside you to make your farms flourish and let clean waters flow; to nourish starved bodies and feed hungry minds. And to those nations like ours that enjoy relative plenty, we say we can no longer afford indifference to the suffering outside our borders, nor can we consume the world's resources without regard to effect. For the world has changed, and we must change with it.

As we consider the role that unfolds before us, we remember with humble gratitude those brave Americans who at this very hour patrol far-off deserts and distant mountains. They have something to tell us, just as the fallen heroes who lie in Arlington whisper through the ages.

We honor them not only because they are the guardians of our liberty, but because they embody the spirit of service – a willingness to find meaning in something greater than themselves.

And yet at this moment, a moment that will define a generation, it is precisely this spirit that must inhabit us all. For as much as government can do, and must do, it is ultimately the faith and determination of the American people upon which this nation relies. It is the kindness to take in a stranger when the levees break, the selflessness of workers who would rather cut their hours than see a friend lose their job which sees us through our darkest hours. It is the firefighter's courage to storm a stairway filled with smoke, but also a parent's willingness to nurture a child that finally decides our fate.

Our challenges may be new. The instruments with which we meet them may be new. But those values upon which our success depends – honesty and hard work, courage and fair play, tolerance and curiosity, loyalty and patriotism – these things are old. These things are true. They have been the quiet force of progress throughout our history.

What is demanded, then, is a return to these truths. What is required of us now is a new era of responsibility – a recognition on the part of every American that we have duties to ourselves, our nation and the world; duties that we do not grudgingly accept, but rather seize gladly, firm in the knowledge that there is nothing so satisfying to the spirit, so defining of our character than giving our all to a difficult task.

This is the price and the promise of citizenship. This is the source of our confidence – the knowledge that God calls on us to shape an uncertain destiny. This is the meaning of our liberty and our creed, why men and women and children of every race and every faith can join in celebration across this magnificent mall; and why a man whose father less than 60 years ago might not have been served in a local restaurant can now stand before you to take a most sacred oath.

So let us mark this day with remembrance of who we are and how far we have traveled. In the year of America's birth, in the coldest of months, a small band of patriots huddled by dying campfires on the shores of an icy river. The capital was abandoned. The enemy was advancing. The snow was stained with blood. At the moment when the outcome of our revolution was most in doubt, the father of our nation ordered these words to be read to the people:

"Let it be told to the future world... that in the depth of winter, when nothing but hope and virtue could survive that the city and the country, alarmed at one common danger, came forth to meet it".

America: In the face of our common dangers, in this winter of our hardship, let us remember these timeless words. With hope and virtue, let us brave once more the icy currents, and endure what storms may come. Let it be said by our children's children that when we were tested we refused to let this journey end, that we did not turn back nor did we falter; and with eyes fixed on the horizon and God's grace upon us, we carried forth that great gift of freedom and delivered it safely to future generations.

Thank you. God bless you. And God bless the United States of America.

Chinese Sample Texts:

胡锦涛在早稻田大学的演讲（2008 年 5 月 8 日）

尊敬的白井克彦校长，尊敬的河野洋平先生，老师们、同学们、朋友们：

首先，我感谢白井克彦校长的邀请。有机会来到著名学府早稻田大学，同青年朋友和老师们相聚一堂，我感到十分高兴。我代表中国人民，向在座各位朋友，向日本人民，表示诚挚问候和良好祝愿！

早稻田大学是中国人民熟悉的学府，与中国有着很深的渊源。早在上世纪初，早稻田大学就招收了数以千计的中国留学生。在中国近代史上有着重要影响的廖仲恺、李大钊、陈独秀、彭湃等曾在这里负笈求学。今天，早稻田大学同中国许多大学和研究机构保持着良好关系、开展着广泛的学术交流，为推动两国人文交流发挥了积极作用。

来到这里，我不禁想起我认识的几位日本朋友，他们是竹下登、海部俊树、小渊惠三、森喜朗、福田康夫、河野洋平先生等。他们都是贵校的校友，为日本发展作出了贡献，也为中日友好事业作出了贡献。在去年早稻田大学建校 125 周年时，你们提出要建设“培养世界人的世界性大学”、“挑战 21 世纪的开放大学”。这符合时代要求。我衷心祝愿贵校培养出更多英才，为日本经济社会发展、为人类进步事业作出更大贡献。

中日是一衣带水的邻邦，两国关系正站在新的历史起点上，面临进一步发展的新机遇。我这次来贵国访问，怀着中国人民对日本人民的友好情谊，带着中国人民对发展中日关系的真诚期待。中国政府和人民真诚希望，同日本政府和人民一道努力，增进互信，加强友谊，深化合作，规划未来，开创中日战略互惠关系全面发展新局面。

老师们、同学们、朋友们！

“世界的道路通向早稻田”，这是早稻田大学的一句名言。我们要推动中日关系长期健康稳定发展、实现两国人民世代友好，就要不断增进两国人民的相互了解。这里，我想从历史和现实的视角谈一谈中国，希望有助于大家更加深入地认识中国。

中国是一个具有悠久历史的国家，也是一个正在发生深刻变革的国家。在5000多年文明发展的漫长进程中，中华民族以勤劳智慧的民族品格、不懈进取的创造活力、自强不息的奋斗精神创造了辉煌的中华文明，为人类文明进步作出了重大贡献。同时，中国也走过了艰难曲折的发展道路。特别是1840年鸦片战争以后，由于封建统治的腐朽没落和帝国主义列强的侵略蹂躏，中国饱经磨难、历经沧桑。为改变受人欺凌、积贫积弱的境遇，实现民族复兴的理想，中国人民奋起抗争、前仆后继、发愤图强。1911年辛亥革命推翻统治中国几千年的君主专制制度以来，中国的发展历程大致可以分为3个阶段。从1911年到1949年，中国人民经过长期浴血奋斗，实现了民族独立和人民解放，建立了人民当家作主的新中国，为实现中国发展繁荣创造了根本条件。从1949年到1978年，中国建立了社会主义制度，实现了历史上最深刻的社会变革，中国人民经过艰辛努力取得了国家建设的巨大成就。从1978年到现在，中国人民毅然决然地踏上改革开放的伟大征程，开始了新的历史条件下新的伟大革命。

今年是中国改革开放30周年，对中国和中国人民来说是一个具有特殊意义的年份。30年来，中国成功实现了从高度集中的计划经济体制到充满活力的社会主义市场经济体制、从封闭半封闭到全方位开放的伟大历史转折，中国经济总量从世界第十一位跃至世界第四位，中国成为世界第三大贸易国，中国人民的生活水平从温饱不足发展到总体小康，中国的面貌发生了历史性变化。

在改革开放的伟大实践中，我们深刻认识到，在当今世界日趋激烈的竞争中，一个国家、一个民族要发展起来，必须锐意改革、着力发展、坚持开放、以人为本、促进和谐。锐意改革，就是要跟上时代潮流，勇于变革、勇于创新，坚决冲破一切妨碍发展的思想观念，坚决改变一切束缚发展的规定和做法，坚决革除一切影响发展的体制弊端，为社会发展进步提供强大动力。着力发展，就是要始终把发展作为第一要务，坚持科学发展，着力把握发展规律、创新发展理念、转变发展方式、破解发展难题，不断解放和发展社会生产力，实现经济社会又好又快发展。坚持开放，就是要打开国门来搞建设，在互利共赢的基础上同所有国家开展经济技术合作，吸收和借鉴人类社会创造的一切优秀文明成果，既通过维护世界和平发展自己，又通过自身发展维护世界和平。以人为本，就是要坚持发展为了人民、发展依靠人民、发展成果由人民共享，尊重人民主体地位，发挥人民首创精神，始终把人民呼声作为第一信号，把人民利益放在第一位置，不断提高人民物质文化生活水平，促进人的全面发展。促进和谐，就是要以解决人民最关心、最直接、最现实的利益问题为重点，着力促进社会公平正义、增强社会创造活力，最大限度增加和谐因素，最大限度减少不和谐因素，确保人民安居乐业、社会安定有序、国家长治久安。

“苟日新，日日新，又日新”。“天行健，君子以自强不息”。这既是中华民族的先哲通过观察宇宙万物提出的重要思想，也深刻揭示了中华民族自强不息的民族精神，因此成为中国的千年传世格言。今天中国人民秉持的价值观念，既来自自己在当今时代的丰富实践，也源于中华文明的深厚根基，成为激励中国人民变革创新、与时俱进的强大精神力量。

总结中国改革开放的历程，中国人民得出了一个不可动摇的结论，这就是：中国过去 30 年的快速发展，靠的是改革开放。中国未来的发展，也必须靠改革开放。改革开放是决定当代中国命运的关键抉择，也是 13 亿中国人民的共同抉择。

我们清醒地认识到，尽管取得了前所未有的发展成就，但中国仍然是世界上最大的发展中国家。中国人口多、底子薄、发展很不平衡，在发展中遇到的矛盾和问题，无论是规模还是复杂性，都是世所罕见的。中国要建成惠及十几亿人口的更高水平的小康社会，要实现现代化、实现全体人民共同富裕，还有很长的路要走，必须持之以恒地艰苦奋斗。

中国将继续沿着中国特色社会主义道路前进。我们将以邓小平理论和“三个代表”重要思想为指导，深入贯彻落实科学发展观，统筹城乡发展、区域发展、经济社会发展、人与自然和谐发展、国内发展和对外开放，更加注重解决民生问题，更加注重增强发展协调性，全面推进经济建设、政治建设、文化建设、社会建设，努力构建生产发展、生活富裕、生态良好的文明发展格局。

中国将始终不渝走和平发展道路。这是中国政府和人民作出的战略抉择。这个战略抉择，立足中国国情，顺应时代潮流，体现了中国对内政策与对外政策的统一、中国人民根本利益与各国人民共同利益的统一，是实现中华民族伟大复兴的必由之路。中国坚定不移地奉行独立自主的和平外交政策，坚定不移地奉行互利共赢的开放战略，致力于推进国际关系民主化，推动经济全球化朝着均衡、普惠、共赢方向发展，促进人类文明交流互鉴，呵护人类赖以生存的地球家园，同世界各国一起分享发展机遇、共同应对风险挑战，推动建设持久和平、共同繁荣的和谐世界。中国奉行防御性的国防政策，不搞军备竞赛，不对任何国家构成军事威胁，永远不称霸，永远不搞扩张。

老师们、同学们、朋友们！

中日两国人民的友好交往绵延2000多年，堪称世界民族交往史上的奇迹。在漫长的历史进程中，中日两国人民相互学习、相互借鉴、相互交融，促进了各自国家发展进步，丰富了东亚文明和世界文明宝库。

到了近代，由于日本军国主义对中国发动侵略战争，两国友好关系受到严重破坏。这段不幸历史，给中华民族造成深重灾难，也使日本人民深受其害。历史是最富哲理的教科书。我们强调牢记历史并不是要延续仇恨，而是要以史为鉴、面向未来，珍爱和平、维护和平，让中日两国人民世世代代友好下去，让各国人民永享太平。

1972 年，中日实现邦交正常化，揭开了两国关系新篇章。从那时以来，中日关系在各个领域都取得长足发展。双边贸易额由实现邦交正常化时的 11 亿美元增加到去年的 2360 亿美元。截至去年年底，两国友好城市达到 236 对，人员往来达到 544 万人次。中日关系的改善和发展，给两国和两国人民带来了实实在在的利益，为促进亚洲和世界的和平与发展作出了重要贡献。

今年是中日和平友好条约缔结 30 周年。在重温中日和平友好条约重大历史意义的时刻，我们深切缅怀那些为中日友好事业呕心沥血、辛勤耕耘的老一辈领导人和各界有识之士，更加感到今天中日友好合作的局面来之不易，值得倍加珍惜。

中日关系正站在新的历史起点上，面临进一步发展的新机遇。随着经济全球化深入发展，中日两国的共同利益不断拓展、合作空间不断扩大，在国际和地区事务中肩负的责任也不断加重。我昨天同福田首相举行了富有成果的会谈。我们就全面深化中日战略互惠关系达成广泛共识，确定了两国关系长期健康稳定发展的总体框架。我们一致同意，双方要共同努力，增进战略互信，深化互利合作，扩大人文交流，推动亚洲振兴，应对全球挑战，共同推进中日战略互惠关系。我愿就这几个问题谈些看法。

第一，增进战略互信。人与人要成为朋友，前提是互信；国与国关系要稳定，基础也在于互信。中日两国都是亚洲和世界的重要国家，双方应该客观认识和正确对待对方发展，相互视为合作双赢的伙伴，而不是零和竞争的对手；相互支持对方和平发展，视对方发展为机遇，而不是威胁；相互尊重对方的重大关切和核心利益，坚持通过对话协商解决分歧。

第二，深化互利合作。中日互为最重要的经贸伙伴。双方应该珍视长期以来两国经贸合作形成的良好格局，充分利用两国经济互补性强、合作潜力大的优越条件，加强两国节能、环保、金融、信息、知识产权保护等重点领域的合作，不断把两国经贸合作提升到更高层次，巩固两国关系的物质基础。

第三，扩大人文交流。人员交往是增进两国人民相互了解的桥梁，文化交流是沟通两国人民感情的渠道。我们应该持之以恒地开展两国人文交流，着力建立两国青少年交流长效机制，夯实中日世代友好的社会基础。

第四，推动亚洲振兴。亚洲振兴离不开中日两国的协调和合作。我们愿同日方及亚洲各国一道努力，推进多种形式的区域、次区域合作，加强共同安全，维护东北亚和平稳定，推进东亚合作进程和东亚共同体建设，在促进亚洲振兴中实现中日共同发展。

第五，应对全球挑战。当今世界面临的共同挑战日益增多，恐怖主义、气候变化、能源安全、粮食安全、金融风险、严重自然灾害、重大传染性疾病、大规模杀伤性武器扩散等影响各国发展和稳定，需要各国携手应对。中国愿同日本一道，积极参与各领域的国际合作，提高协作应对各种挑战的能力，共同推进人类和平与发展的崇高事业。

老师们、同学们、朋友们！

中日友好是两国人民的共同事业，需要两国人民为之不懈努力。通过同日本人民的广泛接触，我深深感到，发展中日友好在日本有着深厚的社会基础。长期以来，日本人民、社会各界和对华友好团体积极推进中日交流，友好合作始终是两国关系发展的主流。在中国现代化建设的进程中，日本政府向中国提供了日元贷款合作，支持中国的基础设施建设、环境保护、能源开发、科技发展，为促进中国现代化建设发挥了积极作用。日本各界友人以不同形式对中国现代化建设提供了热情帮助。对日本众多友好人士为中日友好事业倾注的心血，中国人民将永远铭记。

日本人民善于学习、善于创造，勤劳智慧、奋发向上。远在1400 多年前，日本就先后 20 多次向中国派出遣隋使、遣唐使，借鉴中国的制度、典章、律令，引入佛教、汉字、技术，结合自己的实际形成了独具特色的日本文化。明治维新以后，日本人民努力学习吸收世界先进文明成果，逐步发展成为亚洲第一个现代化国家。日本人民以有限的国土资源创造出举世瞩目的发展成就，日本在制造业、信息、金融、物流等领域位居世界前列，拥有世界一流的节能环保技术。这是日本人民的骄傲，也值得中国人民学习。

这里，我要对两国青年朋友说几句话。曾在贵校学习过的李大钊先生说过，为世界进文明，为人类造幸福，以青春之我，创建青春之人类。两国青年是中日友好的生力军，中日友好的未来要靠你们开创。我曾多年从事青年工作，对青年朋友有着特殊感情。我喜欢同青年朋友们在一起，感受青春的活力，感受生命的火红。1984 年，中国政府邀请 3000 名日本青年访华，举行规模盛大的中日青年友好联欢活动，我全程参加了那次活动，同日本青年朝夕相处，建立了深厚友谊。去年 6 月，我们邀请参加 1984 年中日青年友好联欢活动的日本朋友访华，大家再次欢聚，百感交集。我在致辞中表示："岁月可以改变人们的容颜，但改变不了人间的友情。"这样的经历告诉我，青年时代播下的友谊种子，将永远伴随着我们的人生。我们要共同努力，让中日友好的种子广泛播撒，让中日友好的旗帜代代相传。

今年是中日青少年友好交流年。双方将开展一系列内容丰富、形式多样的友好交流活动。在这里，我愿宣布，中国政府决定邀请100名早稻田大学学生访华。希望在座的青年学生能够加入这一计划，到中国去看一看。

老师们、同学们、朋友们!

再过3个月，第二十九届夏季奥运会将在北京举行。福田首相曾对我谈及日本人民对1964年东京奥运会的真挚情感，闻后感同身受。中国人民真诚希望办好北京奥运会。我们提出“同一个世界，同一个梦想”的口号，就是要通过北京奥运会，光大团结、友谊、和平的奥林匹克精神，增进世界各国人民的相互了解和友谊。借此机会，我愿感谢日本政府和各界人士对北京奥运会筹办的支持，欢迎日本各界朋友到北京观看奥运会，预祝日本体育健儿在北京奥运会上创造佳绩。

老师们、同学们、朋友们!

早稻田戏剧博物馆门楼上嵌刻着莎士比亚的名言“世界是一个大舞台”。古往今来，世界大舞台上演出的所有戏剧，主角始终都是各国人民。我衷心期望，中日两国人民手牵手、肩并肩，在中日合作的大舞台上，在振兴亚洲、促进世界和平与发展的大舞台上，共同创造中日关系更加美好的明天，共同创造世界更加美好的明天!

谢谢大家。

胡锦涛在澳门特别行政区第三届政府就职典礼上的讲话(2009年12月20日)

同胞们，朋友们:

今天，我们怀着喜悦的心情，在这里隆重庆祝澳门回归祖国10周年。10年前的今天，中葡两国政府举行了澳门政权交接仪式，中国政府庄严宣告对澳门恢复行使主权，中华人民共和国澳门特别行政区成立。澳门回归祖国，实现了包括广大澳门同胞在内的全国各族人民的夙愿，标志着澳门同胞从此真正成为这块土地上的主人，澳门从此进入历史发展新纪元。这是中华民族发展史上的一座重要里程碑。

在这里，我代表中央政府和全国各族人民，向全体澳门市民，致以诚挚的问候！向新就任的澳门特别行政区行政长官崔世安先生和特别行政区主要官员、行政会委员，表示热烈的祝贺！

我相信，新一届澳门特别行政区政府一定能够总结经验、继往开来，团结带领广大澳门市民把澳门建设得更加美好！

此时此刻，我们要向创造性地提出“一国两制”科学构想、为澳门回归祖国开辟了正确道路的邓小平先生，表示深深的怀念！向为实现澳门顺利交接和成功落实“一国两制”作出了历史性贡献的江泽民先生，致以崇高的敬意！借此机会，我们还要向所有关心澳门、为澳门保持繁荣稳定作出贡献的海内外同胞和国际友人，表示衷心的感谢！

澳门回归祖国 10 年来，在中央政府和祖国内地大力支持下，澳门特别行政区行政长官何厚铧先生和特区政府带领澳门各界人士团结奋斗、务实进取，积极应对亚洲金融危机、非典疫情、国际金融危机等带来的严峻挑战，努力克服澳门发展进程中遇到的种种困难，保持澳门繁荣稳定，各项事业取得长足进步，使澳门这座历史悠久的商埠名城焕发出前所未有的生机活力。“一国两制”在澳门的成功实践，为澳门发展谱写出新的辉煌篇章，为国家发展增添了夺目光彩！

澳门回归祖国以来的 10 年，是“一国两制”在澳门成功实践的 10 年，是澳门基本法顺利实施的 10 年，也是澳门各界人士积极探索符合澳门实际的发展道路、不断取得进步的 10 年。回顾澳门回归祖国 10 年来的不平凡历程，可以得出以下重要启示。

第一，必须全面准确理解和贯彻“一国两制”方针。“一国两制”是一个完整的概念，“一国”和“两制”紧密相连。要全面准确理解和贯彻“一国两制”方针，关键是要把爱国和爱澳有机统一起来。既要维护澳门原有的社会经济制度、生活方式，又要维护国家主权、统一、安全，尊重国家主体实行的社会主义制度；既要维护澳门特别行政区依法享有的高度自治权，充分保障澳门同胞当家作主的主人翁地位，又要尊重中央政府依法享有的权力，坚决反对任何外部势力干预澳门事务。今年年初，澳门基本法第二十三条立法顺利完成，充分体现了澳门特别行政区政府、立法会和澳门各界人士对维护国家安全和利益的高度责任感，也为澳门长治久安提供了坚实保障。只要澳门同胞继续发扬光荣传统，在爱国爱澳旗帜下实现最广泛的团结，就一定能够构筑起澳门长期繁荣稳定的牢固政治基础。

第二，必须严格依照澳门基本法办事。澳门基本法在澳门特别行政区法律体系中具有最高地位。依法治澳，就是要按照澳门基本法办事，坚决维护澳门基本法的权威。澳门回归祖国以来，特别行政区政府和各社会团体坚持不懈宣传推广澳门基本法，自觉以澳门基本法规范行政、立法、司法行为和处理政制发展等重大问题。这是澳门特别行政区10年来所取得的一项重要成就。要在这一基础上进一步健全澳门特别行政区各项法律法规，加强制度建设，特别是要按照以人为本、勤政、廉洁、高效的要求，完善政府行政规章制度，促进澳门特别行政区政府管治水平不断提高。

第三，必须集中精力推动发展。发展是硬道理。澳门特别行政区政府和社会各界人士在过去10年中始终牢牢把握发展这个主题，避免政治纷争和社会内耗，形成了经济快速增长、民生明显改善的良好局面。在今后的发展中，要更加注重集民智、聚民心、汇民力，更加注重发展的全面性、协调性、可持续性，切实提高澳门抵御各种经济金融风险能力。当前，特别要充分利用中央政府已经采取的一系列支持澳门发展的政策措施以及国家颁布实施《珠江三角洲地区改革发展规划纲要》、《横琴总体发展规划》的有利机遇，加强同内地特别是广东省的合作。要继续加强和完善对博彩业的管理，努力推动澳门经济适度多元发展。要统筹规划，加大教育、科技、文化、卫生、体育等社会事业投入，使发展成果惠及广大澳门市民，致力于提高市民生活综合素质，促进澳门经济社会全面协调可持续发展。

第四，必须坚持维护社会和谐稳定。澳门是一个多元化社会。各阶层各界别虽然利益多元、诉求多样，但根本利益是一致的。良好的治安环境、融洽的社会氛围、稳定的发展局面是澳门全社会的共同福祉。包容共济是促进澳门社会和谐稳定的良方益策。澳门同胞向来讲团结、重协商，只要大家在维护澳门长期繁荣稳定的大目标下相互尊重、求同存异、加强沟通、顾全大局，就一定能够找到解决矛盾和问题的办法，为澳门各项事业发展营造良好社会氛围。

第五，必须着力培养各类人才。人才是各项事业发展之本。不断提升澳门竞争力，最关键的支撑因素是人才。要着眼长远，增强紧迫感，大力发展教育、科技、文化事业，培养造就一大批澳门社会发展需要的政治人才、经济人才、专业技术人才以及其他各方面人才。要高度重视和加强爱国爱澳优秀年轻人才培养，使澳门同胞素有的爱国爱澳传统薪火相传、发扬光大，使“一国两制”事业后继有人。

同胞们、朋友们！

“一国两制”事业是香港特别行政区、澳门特别行政区和祖国内地共同发展繁荣的事业，也是中华民族伟大复兴事业的重要组成部分。在已经取得成功经验的基础上，把这一伟大事业继续推向前进，需要中央政府和香港特别行政区政府、澳门特别行政区政府以及社会各界人士共同努力。在这里，我郑重重申，中央政府将继续坚定不移贯彻“一国两制”、“港人治港”、“澳人治澳”、高度自治的方针，严格按照香港基本法、澳门基本法办事，全力支持香港特别行政区、澳门特别行政区行政长官和特区政府依法施政。中央政府对香港、澳门采取的任何方针政策措施，都会始终坚持有利于保持香港、澳门长期繁荣稳定，有利于增进香港、澳门全体市民福祉，有利于推动香港、澳门和国家共同发展的原则。伟大的祖国始终是香港、澳门繁荣稳定的坚强后盾。

同胞们、朋友们！

新中国成立60年来，经过包括澳门同胞在内的全国各族人民共同奋斗，国家建设取得了举世瞩目的伟大成就，综合国力大幅增强，人民生活显著改善，国际地位和影响空前提高。国际金融危机发生以来，我国各族人民坚定信心、团结奋斗、共克时艰，取得了应对国际金融危机冲击、保持经济平稳较快发展的显著成绩。当前，全国各族人民正沿着中国特色社会主义道路，继续解放思想，坚持改革开放，推动科学发展，促进社会和谐，继续为建设惠及十几亿人口的更高水平的小康社会而奋斗，继续朝着建设富强民主文明和谐的社会主义现代化国家、实现中华民族伟大复兴的宏伟目标奋勇前进。

澳门同胞既是澳门特别行政区的主人，也是国家的主人。澳门特别行政区成立以来，不仅从祖国内地快速发展中获得了源源不竭的发展动力和越来越多的发展机遇，在国际上分享着伟大祖国的尊严和荣耀，也为国家发展作出了重要贡献。对澳门同胞长期以来为国家改革开放和社会主义现代化建设、为祖国和平统一大业作出的重要贡献，全国各族人民不会忘记。

展望未来，我们坚信，澳门的明天与伟大祖国一样，一定会更加美好！澳门同胞的未来生活与全国各族人民一样，一定会更加幸福！

谢谢大家。